Battlegrou

MONTA

Other guides in the Battleground Europe Series:

Walking the Salient *by* Paul Reed
Ypres - Sanctuary Wood and Hooge *by* Nigel Cave
Ypres - Hill 60 *by* Nigel Cave
Ypres - Messines Ridge *by* Peter Oldham

Walking the Somme *by* Paul Reed
Somme - Gommecourt *by* Nigel Cave
Somme - Serre *by* Jack Horsfall & Nigel Cave
Somme - Beaumont Hamel *by* Nigel Cave
Somme - Thiepval *by* Michael Stedman
Somme - La Boisselle *by* Michael Stedman
Somme - Fricourt *by* Michael Stedman
Somme - Delville Wood *by* Nigel Cave
Somme - Pozieres *by* Graham Keech
Somme - Courcelette *by* Paul Reed
Somme - Boom Ravine *by* Trevor Pidgeon
Somme - Mametz Wood *by* Michael Renshaw

Arras - Vimy Ridge *by* Nigel Cave
Arras - Bullecourt *by* Graham Keech

Hindenburg Line *by* Peter Oldham
Epehy *by* Bill Mitchenson
Riqueval *by* Bill Mitchenson

Boer War - The Relief of Ladysmith, Colenso, Spion Kop *by* Lewis Childs

Accrington Pals Trail *by* WilliamTurner

Poets at War: Wilfred Owen *by* Helen McPhail and Philip Guest

Gallipoli *by* Nigel Steel

Battleground Europe Series guides in preparation:
Ypres - Polygon Wood *by* Nigel Cave
La Basseé - Givenchy *by* Michael Orr
La Basseé - Neuve Chapelle 1915 *by* Geoff Bridger
Walking Arras *by* Paul Reed
Arras - Monchy le Preux *by* Colin Fox
Somme - Following the Ancre *by* Michael Stedman
Somme - High Wood *by* Terry Carter
Somme - Advance to Victory 1918 *by* Michael Stedman
Somme - Ginchy *by* Michael Stedman
Somme - Combles *by* Paul Reed
Somme - Beaucourt *by* Michael Renshaw

Walking Verdun *by* Paul Reed

Poets at War: Edmund Blunden *by* Helen McPhail and Philip Guest

Boer War - The Siege of Ladysmith *by* Lewis Childs
Isandhlwana *by* Ian Knight and Ian Castle
Rorkes Drift *by* Ian Knight and Ian Castle

With the continued expansion of the Battleground series a Battleground Europe Club has been formed to benefit the reader. The purpose of the Club is to keep members informed of new titles and key developments by way of a quarterly newsletter, and to offer many other reader-benefits. Membership is free and by registering an interest you can help us predict print runs and thus maintain prices at their present levels. Please call the office 01226 734555, or send your name and address along with a request for more information to:

Battleground Europe Club
Pen & Sword Books Ltd, 47 Church Street, Barnsley, South Yorkshire S70 2AS

Battleground Europe

MONTAUBAN

Graham Maddocks

Series editor
Nigel Cave

LEO COOPER

This work is dedicated to
Diane Morley
Colleague and Friend,
without whose professional advice, encourgement
and help it would have been impossible to write.

First published in 1999 by
LEO COOPER
an imprint of
Pen Sword Books Limited
47 Church Street, Barnsley, South Yorkshire S70 2AS

ISBN 0 85052 579 9

A CIP catalogue of this book is available
from the British Library

Printed by St Edmundsbury Press Limited
Bury St Edmunds, Suffolk

For up-to-date information on other titles produced under the Leo Cooper imprint,
please telephone or write to:
Pen & Sword Books Ltd, FREEPOST, 47 Church Street
Barnsley, South Yorkshire S70 2AS
Telephone 01226 734222

CONTENTS

The Madonna of Mountauban still intact in 1916 just after the capture of
the village. British soldiers excavate an unexploded British howitzer shell
at the base.

INTRODUCTION BY
SERIES EDITOR

With this addition to the series, the old Front Line of 1 July 1916 has been completely covered south of the Albert-Bapaume Road. Graham Maddocks has been deeply involved in this sector; he is the author of the Liverpool Pals, who fought their first great battle here, and presided over the committee that raised the memorial to the Liverpool and Manchester Pals in the village.

Montauban was one of the rare places on the Somme where British endeavours were rewarded with success – in some cases, more than had been anticipated. One of the reasons for this lay in the German intelligence analysis, which reckoned that the British onslaught would fall from Gommecourt to just south of Fricourt, so that their resources, in particular engineering resources, were dedicated there. This goes some way to explaining the almost complete lack of success to the north; but it should not in any way detract from what was achieved by these soldiers from a nation which had so little continental military tradition behind it.

This book is considerably enhanced by the amount of work that Mr Maddocks has put into the early days of the war around Montauban, so that the fierce fighting which involved the French army as the line was being stabilised in autumn 1914 gets coverage. Too often we British tend to take the Somme battlefield as ours, and neglect the role of France. French soldiers bore the brunt of the war for its first two years, and the relevant chapter in this book is a timely reminder of that. One hopes that the notable efforts of the French Sixth Army, to the right of the British positions here at Montauban, will also be covered in depth at some stage. Graham Maddocks also gives an interesting account of the opponents of the British at Montauban, that extraordinarily effective fighting machine, the Imperial German Army. Whilst we neglect the French in our studies, we also neglect the Germans as well, and one has to face the fact that one of the reasons we had so many casualties was because of the tenacity and the ability to withstand punishment that was such a characteristic of the German soldier.

Visitors will find a wealth of detail and excellent walks in an area not overfull of remnants of this great conflict, which will help them to appreciate the achievement of the British soldier in this, the most successful part of the attack of 1 July, 1916.

Nigel Cave, *Ely Place, London*

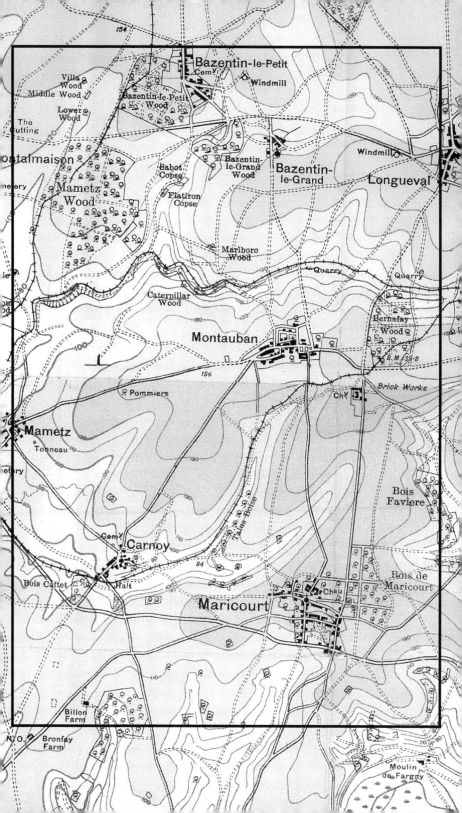

INTRODUCTION

The story of the Battle of the Somme and more particularly its first day, are well known by the majority of the British public; in fact, it is ingrained into the folk memory of the British nation - yet the vast majority of its people have either gained the wrong impression of it, or are content to believe the oft-wheeled-out myths concerning it.

Popular belief holds that not only was it the most disastrous day in the history of the British Army - (in terms of disaster, the fall of Singapore in 1942 was actually much worse) - but that it was a total failure, wiping out the flower of British manhood for the gain of absolutely nothing.

It is fairly easy to see how this myth gained root - especially when one views the slaughter of some units on that sunny July morning in the third year of the war - slaughter without a shred of success. Curiously, often coupled with this myth is the equally false notion that all the men were brave heroes and all their officers, (especially the generals), incompetent buffoons!

Whilst it is not the purpose of this book to explore this hypothesis - it has been quite adequately deliberated over elsewhere - Montauban will nevertheless destroy a few well held beliefs as well as shattering a few myths. Even the mystique and magic of the date of the opening of the battle is confused in the minds of many. How often do we hear that 1 July was 'the middle day of the middle year of the war', for instance? In point of fact, 1916 was a leap year and thus had 366 days, so there was no middle day that year and in true calendar terms, the Great War might have spanned five years, but only lasted for just over four - so there was no middle year of the war either!

In many ways, the battle for Montauban is unique in the long struggle of the Battle of the Somme - the most obvious reason being that the village was the only one captured on schedule on 1 July, and the hopes and planning of 1 July were totally justified in military terms at Montauban. However, despite the delight it gave to British propaganda, the scale of the success there was soon lost to the grieving public as any euphoria which had accompanied the victory gave way to a chilling numbness. Once the terrible consequences of the attack further north became known, even the remarkable recovery and successes of the British Army on 2 July could not prevent the creeping realisation that it was not going to be an easy victory.

Nevertheless, what can never be disputed is the success of the 18th and 30th Divisions on that day – although even after the passage of more than eighty years, this is still not a well known or accepted fact. Despite obvious and catastrophic set-backs, the men of these two divisions accomplished near miracles over difficult and varying terrain and even though it is odious to compare their success with the total failure elsewhere, it is that very failure that has fuelled the public's perception of the Somme battle ever since.

Who would readily believe, for instance, that a largely citizen army – composed mainly of men who had been civilians just two years earlier, albeit 'stiffened' by Regular Army battalions – could trounce the best of Germany's might, who were professional, experienced and hitherto victorious?

Who would readily believe, also, that a battalion of 89 Brigade could capture all its objectives without actually losing a single soldier in action? It does seem impossible to a public conditioned to accept that all the attackers on the first day of the Somme gained no ground at all, yet were still wiped out, almost to a man – but it did happen.

It was the men of General Congreve's XIII Corps attacking up the slopes of the Montauban Ridge that unseated a resolute German Army – a brilliant Army which had had twenty-one months to prepare for that inevitable day.

Their battle was virtually won on that July morning and certainly by the following day, they had ensured that the once red-roofed village of Montauban was safely back in allied hands and would never again have to suffer the agony and despoilation that became the routine fate of many other villages on the Somme.

When the author made his first pilgrimage to the Somme area in 1972 there were very few British visitors to the area, as most of the survivors were by then too old, and their sons and daughters had not yet retired and felt the need to research their family histories. Only devotees and serious students seemed to make visits. In fact, returning there for his next visit in 1973, (and every year since), the author was shocked to find that in some cemetery visitors' books, his name from the previous year was the last one to be written!

For a variety of reasons, this is not now the case and there is a flourishing trade in commemorative visits as many thousands each year make regular pilgrimages. Whilst it is most important that the men buried there should never be forgotten, some could be forgiven for seeing these visits as a double-edged sword. For others, the Somme battle has engendered almost a cult of remembrance and the 1 July anniversary can not be allowed to pass without hordes of them, some curiously dressed in Great War period uniform, eating corned beef and sipping tots of rum, before prancing over the battlefields at 7.30 in the morning (modern French time, of course).

Unfortunately, also, too many will have seen badly behaved British school children swarming all over the battlefield areas, seemingly out of control and without any idea of why they are there or what happened to their ancestors on the same spots! Perhaps the author should take some of the blame for this, however, as it was he who wrote in the 1970s, the first school battlefield tours for the market leader in school travel. There are, of course, equally many well organised school parties whose pupils are moved by the sacrifices made on their behalfs and who are properly taught about the importance of the places they visit.

Other unsavoury cults which have developed in recent years include the desecration of headstones with crayon, ink or simply mud, the better that they might be photographed and a macabre and singular preoccupation with visiting the graves of those executed for cowardice and desertion. These visitors do not seem content merely to pay homage to those men, most of whom at least had a choice in whether they lived or died, - unlike their countless thousands of dead comrades, killed in action or died of wounds. They seem to have a smug fixation that everyone else, – through often over-large entries in the cemetery visitors' books – should also appreciate their contrived opinions and applaud their 1990s political concern.

After much reflection, however, one is tempted to ask if it really matters why people visit the graves of the fallen and what they do when they get there? Those who alone have the right to judge can not speak any more and the mere fact that visitors are increasing in numbers each year will ensure that when all those who remember the dead have themselves passed away, their countrymen will continue to honour a generation lost because it was unlucky enough to have been born at the latter end of the Victorian age.

On the right is a sketch of the original grave of Sgt 164141 Albert Edward Gray, a great uncle of the author at Ste Marie Cemetery Le Havre. Today *(left)* it has a CWGC headstone, but this bears the badge of the regular battalions of the King's Regiment, not the Pals. Sgt Gray was mortally wounded on 8 July 1916 by the same shell which killed the battalion commander, Lieut Col E H Trotter.

ACKNOWLEDGEMENTS

Individuals

This book, like all others of a similar nature could never have been written without the help of a vast number of people, all of whom freely gave their time, help and often expertise. I would especially like to thank the following, mentioned in alphabetical order as it would be impossible to put their help in any kind of 'order of merit'

Nigel Cave the series editor for patience, forbearance and advice!

Martin Middlebrook the celebrated expert and author on the Battle of the Somme who most kindly agreed to my using extracts from his widely known and acclaimed *First Day on the Somme*, both those already published and some he had researched but did not actually use.

Pupils of The Mosslands School, Wallasey and Park High School, Birkenhead, who helped out with research in many small ways on school trips to the Somme in October 1996 and 1997.

Mike Stedman, the prolific book writer and Somme expert, who also allowed me to use extracts from his book *Manchester Pals* and freely offered advice and encouragement from the early research stages of this work.

Peter Threlfall, friend and Great War devotee who offered his usual encouragement and enthusiasm and searched through his extensive collection of postcards to find suitable material for inclusion.

Ray Westlake well known author of many books on The Great War who tirelessly searched through his extensive library to find appropriate volumes and Battalion War Diaries for me to use and then photocopied them to make my research even easier!

The French Connection

Il aurait été impossible de prérarer un ouvrage racontant l'histoire d'un village de la Somme sans la coopération la plus intime des autochtones. En conséquence je voudrais surtout remercier:-

Monsieur et Madame Gérard Driencourt-Brule pour leur amitié et leur aide. J'ai rencontré les Driencourts pour la première fois pendant que je cherchais à placer le monument consacré aux Liverpool and Manchester Pals. Leur famille a généreusement fait don de la parcelle sur laquelle le monument est actuellement situé. Gérard Driencourt, maire adjoint de Montauban, m'a obtenu également des renseignements et des photos d'une grande valeur et il m'a toujours accueilli comme un membre de la famille pendant mes nombreuses visites de recherche à la Somme.

Jean-Pierre Matte, du Musée des Abris, Albert, pour avoir fourni des photos de Montauban pendant et après la Grande Guerre et la plupart des renseignements sur la bataille pour Montauban en 1914.

Pierre Lavoisier, Jean-Paul Julien et Xavier Mauro de l'Aéro Club Maurice Weiss d'Albert, qui m'ont aidé à réaliser une ambition longtemps chérie de survoler les vieux champs de bataille de la Somme à la hauteur d'un avion de la Grande Guerre et de prendre des photos de la région où le Corps XIII britannique a fait bataille.

Michel Duthoit et Monsieur et Madame Daudigny Duthoit du Grand Hôtel de la Paix, Albert et Gilbert Froment, Maire de Montauban.

The following have also given help in a variety of ways:-

Marion E. Arnold, M.A. Bennett, Dawn Birkinshaw, Paul Campbell, David Cliffe, David S. Cousins, Joe Devereux, Tim Everson, David Evans, George and Ian of Fotokam, Birkenhead, Colin Fox, Jim Furlong, the late Charles Heaton, Leigh Hewitt, Penelope James, Christel Pobgee, Kathryn Pryor, Bruce Purvis, Major J.C. Rogerson, Jeff Scully, Judy Smith, Margaret Smith, Linda and Tony Swift, Louisa Steel, Derek Sheard, Angie Simpson, Barry Stephenson, J.A. Theobald, Vic Thompson, Alex Tomeny, Greg Ward, Joseph T. Warden, Gary Wimpress, Crispin Worthington, and Lieutenant Colonel L.M.B. Wilson, M.B.E..

Institutions

Bedford Central Library, Canterbury Library, Chelmsford Central Library, Chichester Public Library, The Imperial War Museum, The Mitchell Library, Glasgow, Kingston Museum and Heritage Centre, Maidstone Library, Manchester Central Library, Ministère des Anciens Combattants, et Victimes de Guerre, Paris, Musée des Abris, Albert, Norfolk Studies Library, Northampton Central Library, The Queen's Royal Surrey Regiment Museum, Princess of Wales Royal Regimental Museum, Reading County Reference Library, Regimental Museum, The Princess of Wales's Royal Regiment and Queen's Regiment, Richmond Library, The Royal Logistic Corps Museum, Salisbury Reference Library, The Royal Scots Fusiliers Regimental Museum, Glasgow, Suffolk Record Office, Surrey Local Studies Library, Guildford.

HOW TO USE THIS BOOK

Very few if any pilgrims to the Western Front ever visit a battlefield completely 'cold' – the visit is usually for a specific purpose such as to seek out the grave of a relative or discover where he or his unit had fought. To this extent, most visitors will have already done some preliminary research, if only to ascertain to which unit an individual belonged.

The obvious starting point for such a search is the soldier's family and it is surprising what family archives and family memories can turn up. If the soldier was known to have died as a result of the Great War, then the normal next line of research should be The Commonwealth War Graves Commission, at 2, Marlow Road, Maidenhead, Berkshire, Telephone 01628 634221. If he survived, then it is more difficult to trace his personal details, but if you know he was involved in the Battle of the Somme and more hopefully, the battle at Montauban, there might be documents still extant that might verify that. If all the proof of his service that has survived is his cap badge or a photograph of him in uniform, and you are still sure that he was involved in the battle at Montauban, this book should tell you his unit and where he actually fought.

At this stage, it is worth trying to discover the regimental museum which covers the unit in which he served and then writing to its curator to see if the museum holds a copy of the Battalion War Diary for that period. A good source for regimental museums is *A Guide to Military Museums* by Terence Wise, (see the Bibliography). It is always a good idea to enclose a stamped self-addressed envelope and a promise to pay any photocopying or research fees! If the soldier was an other rank, there is unlikely to be a mention of him personally in the War Diary, but it will give you an extra link with the past. If the soldier was an officer, then there is more chance that he will be mentioned, especially if he was wounded or killed and his military papers might also be amongst those recently released by the Public Record Office at Richmond, and are certain to be there, whatever his rank, if he was wounded or was in receipt of a pension.

It is possible at this stage that The Imperial War Museum or The National Army Museum might have extra information about his unit that might help – it is always worth while letting them know what information you have and asking if they have anything else. If you know where the soldier lived at the time of his enlistment, a search through the local papers at about the time he enlisted or anything from a week after the first day of the Somme battle up until a couple of months later might also pay dividends.

Although it is possible in good weather to visit the Somme battlefields on foot or by bicycle, having arrived by train from Calais to Albert, a car nevertheless gives more flexibility and, especially if shared with friends, can be a fairly cheap way of making a pilgrimage – especially out of season when most ferry companies or the Channel Tunnel give better rates. Most Sunday newspapers or the teletext services are very helpful for getting the best deals. Insurance is a must – both for vehicle and passengers and although the possession of an E 111 (obtained from any Post Office) will ensure that you will get medical treatment if in need, you will still have to pay for it on the spot and then claim it back in England. A private company medical insurance certificate usually gets round this problem. Although European Union membership has made travel on the Continent much easier and a green card insurance document for your car is no longer mandatory, it is still much easier, should you be unlucky enough to have an accident, if you have obtained one before leaving Great Britain.

Albert is the best centre for a tour of the Montauban battlefields and

is particularly appropriate for a visitor to those parts, as most troops going up the line would have passed through the town first. Now, as then, the town is dominated by the Basilica of Notre-Dame de Brebières, surmounted by a gleaming gold leaf statue of the Virgin Mary holding aloft the infant Jesus. The present statue is not the original, but was replaced when the basilica was rebuilt after the Great War. The Germans shelled the tower in 1914 as it was being used as an observation post by the French and the Madonna figure was tilted over at an angle of 90 degrees to the base. An Allied soldiers' legend quickly grew that when the Virgin fell, the war would end and first French and later British engineers secured it to the base in case the legend was fulfilled too early! The Germans also maintained a legend, but this stated that whichever nation toppled the statue would lose the war.

Thereafter, the statue became a symbol to soldiers all over the Somme front on both sides, as they could see it gleaming brightly in the sunshine from their earth-bound abodes. Eventually, in 1918 after the British had

The restored Madonna and Child. Note the devastated area below.

abandoned Albert to the Germans during the March retreat, it was shelled and toppled – by the British. The war ended months later so perhaps the legend had come true – but not the German version!

The original statue was still to be seen just inside the re-built basilica as another generation of British troops retreated once more from the Germans – in 1940, in another war. Perhaps not taking any more chances, the Germans exported it to the Fatherland where it was melted down for scrap!

The basilica is an excellent place to start any tour of the Montauban battlefields, although there is very little inside – just a faded painting - to show the wartime history of the place and the fact that it was used as a casualty clearing station at one stage in the battle.

Another good starting place for visitors is the Musée des Abris (The Museum of Shelters) whose entrance is just to the right of the basilica. It is a truly magnificent museum which leads the visitor right underneath the town and out into the nearby park, via a visitors' centre, where genuine battlefield souvenirs and relics can be bought at reasonable prices. Along the way, however, are many static displays placed in vaults in the walls, containing uniforms, insignia, arms and ammunition from all the armies which fought there. There is also a video showing continuously, which tells the story of the Somme battlefields.

Although there is four and five star accommodation available in nearby Arras, Amiens and Péronne, for closeness to the battlefields and the sheer charm of the town, a stay in Albert is highly

Albert Basilica as it appeared at the close of 1917, showing the famous virgin suspended in mid-air.

recommended. An advance telephone call to the Office de Tourisme, (Tourist Office) at 9 Rue Gambetta, Telephone 00 333 22 75 16 42 or a visit on arrival – it is situated virtually opposite the basilica - is often a good idea as the office can tell you what is available at that time and make a booking for you if necessary. Otherwise, hotels within the town of Albert are :

Le Royal Picardie ***, Route d'Amiens, 80300 Albert,
Telephone 00 333 22 75 37 00, Fax 00 333 22 75 60 19
Hôtel de la Basilique **, 3, Rue Gambetta, 80300 Albert,
Telephone 00 333 22 75 10 47, Fax 00 333 22 75 10 47
Le Relais Fleuri **, 56, Avenue Faidherbe, 80300 Albert,
Telephone 00 333 22 75 08 11, Fax 00 333 22 74 02 75
Grand Hôtel de la Paix *, 39, Rue Victor Hugo, 8030, Albert,
Telephone 00 333 22 75 01 64, Fax 00 333 22 75 44 17
Hôtel du Nord, 48, Avenue de la République, 80300, Albert,
Telephone 00 333 22 75 08 84
Le Snooker, 2, Place de la Gare, 80300, Albert,
Telephone 00 333 22 74 73 99

The Office de Tourisme also has lists of French-run bed and breakfast accommodation and gites (houses for rent) in the area. The following hotels/guest houses in the immediate area are run by British people who are naturally most sympathetic to the Great War student and visitor :

Les Galets, Route de Beaumont, 80560, Auchonvillers,
Telephone/Fax 00 333 22 76 28 79
Avril Williams, 10, Rue de Lattre, 80560, Auchonvillers,
Telephone 00 333 22 76 23 66
Sommecourt, 39, Grande Rue, 80300, Courcellette,
Telephone/Fax 00 333 22 74 01 35
Journey's End, 3, Rue de la Place, Hardecourt-Aux-Bois,
Telephone 00 333 22 85 17 68

Once you have visited Albert, you can decide which part of the battlefield to visit first. Wherever you decide to go, you should have read Martin Middlebrook's *The First Day on the Somme*, which is probably the best book written on the topic. It is hard to realise that it was first researched nearly thirty years ago when many of the participants in the Battle for Montauban were still alive and lucid in memory. Since its publication in 1972, not only is it still the 'bible' for Somme travellers, but it has introduced countless thousands of mildly interested people to the history of their ancestors and turned them into devoted enthusiasts.

By now you will know exactly why you wish to visit the battlefields of Montauban and whatever your reasoning, it is probably a good idea to begin with Tour One – A General Circuit of the 18th and 30th Division Attack Area, from Chapter Three. Using the maps and information specified, it will not take you long to gain an affinity with the area and a desire to take this further. If there is a specific place you want to visit, which you will have found in Chapters Two and Three, now is the time to seek it out. Unless you are a real enthusiast, you will probably not want to read through Chapter Two in one sitting, but instead discover the parts which interest you particularly and then explore them, taking in at the same time what exactly happened there. After this, if you have the time and the inclination, explore the rest of the tours to familiarise yourself with the whole of the success of XIII Corps on 1 July 1916. However you plan your visit, you should make time to explore the memorials and monuments shown in Chapter Four.

Before you leave the Somme, you should also find time to visit The Memorial to the Missing at Thiepval to pay especial homage to those men of XIII Corps who ensured the victory on that fateful day, but paid with their lives and their identities.

Although not really part of XIII Corps area, another worthwhile visit before turning for home would be to Delville Wood – shrine and memorial to South Africa's involvement in the wars of the twentieth century, There you will find a spectacular memorial and purpose built museum and a warm and friendly welcome from Tom and Janet Fairgrieve. You will also be able to buy refreshments and reasonably priced genuine battlefield souvenirs and relics from the shop attached to the museum.

If it is your first visit to the Somme, you are to be envied, because the first visit is one to be remembered for all time. The things to see and remember around the Montauban battlefields are so numerous and varied that you will probably not be able to take them all in at once, but by using this guide, you will be able to make a fairly intensive visit in a fairly short time. Perhaps almost as pleasurable as your first sight of Montauban, high up on the ridge, will be all the follow up study at home. There, you will take out your photographs, look once more at your maps and re-discover what happened at the exact spot that you can remember standing upon.

Once more you will remember what it was that drew you to that little Picardy village and begin to formulate plans for your return – for no-one ever goes to Montauban only once – not today anyway!

Chapter One

PREPARATIONS AND COMBATANTS

The French

The village of Montauban-de-Picardie has existed as a settlement since prehistoric times, as the high ridge it sits upon makes it an excellent defensive position. Certainly its coat of arms is known to have existed 'from time immemorial', but dates back at least to the Crusades of the 11th Century.

he Arms of Iontauban

In the early 12th Century, the village was known as Vadencourt although it was situated slightly further south of today's village. One hundred years later, it was renamed Mont-Alba and became Mons Albanus shortly afterwards. Both these titles mean white mound or white mountain. By the end of the century, the title Montauban was being used.

The Hundred Years' War, which lasted from 1337 until 1453, saw the complete destruction of the original village by the British and it was later rebuilt on its present site. During this time, Bertrand de Montauban, one of the principal knights of the Duke of Aquitaine was killed at the Battle of Agincourt in 1415 and in 1430, Hector de Folvy took on the title Lord of Montauban. He married Marie de Colleville and they had two sons, Guy and Thibaud. The latter became Lord of Montauban and Conseiller-Chambellan to King Charles VIII, who reigned from 1483 to 1498. Tradition has it that King Louis XIV 'Le Roi Soleil' visited the village in 1670 when it comprised 412 inhabitants and 60 houses.

Like most rural villages in the area, from mediaeval times onwards, Montauban had a flourishing cottage industry producing woven cloth, but this diminished with the coming of the industrial revolution and factory production to the Somme. Thus, although some fifty families were still producing cloth in 1850, they had completely disappeared by 1900. Certainly by the outbreak of the Great War, the main produce of the area was agricultural, facilitated by Montauban's vast fields and fertile soil.

The Great War first came to the village in late August 1914 following the Battle of Le Cateau on the 26th. The British and German Armies had separated and as the Allies fell back to defend Paris, von Kluck's First German Army swung across to the north. His IV Reserve

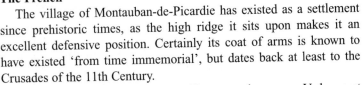

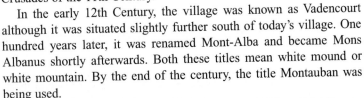

18

General von Kluck

Corps moved into the Somme area from the east, through Montauban and having taken Albert, turned south through Amiens to fight the Battle of the Marne. When this resulted in stalemate, both sides began the race to the sea, in order to control the Channel Ports and the Germans returned to the Somme and began to hold and fortify the high ground. Because of its prominence on the ridge, Montauban was taken and by the end of September, the French Army moved to re-capture its dominating position.

On 26 September, at about mid-day, the three battalions of the French 69e Régiment d'Infanterie arrived in the area from Eclusiers, Suzanne and Bray sur Somme. The regiment, from the province of Lorraine, was part of the 11th Division of the XXth Army Corps. Just before the outbreak of war, it had left its barracks at Essey, near Nancy

Map showing the area fought over by the French 69e R I on the Somme in 1914.

A tribute to the 69e and 269e and 42e RI for their service in the Great War.

in the Département Meurthe-et-Moselle, and had fought with great distinction in the Lorraine region, during August, especially at Morhange and Grand-Couronné. By mid-September, it had moved into Picardy and the Somme.

One soldier of the regiment, who took part in the struggle for Montauban, Sergent Fourrier (Quartermaster-Sergeant) Gabolde, later told of its exploits in the area:[1]

Commandant Ducrot [2] and the liaison officer of the 1st Battalion spent the night of the 24th/25th September in a large haystack outside Bray-sur-Somme. Throughout the day of the 25th, the guns rumbled dully towards Contalmaison and the battalion waited in the meadows for the moment when it would be engaged in the battle which was taking place on the plateaux and in the marshes which surround the meandering river.

On 26 September, at about mid-day, the regiment assembled in a wood, south of Carnoy.[3] In the afternoon it was ordered to occupy the village of Maricourt to the east of Carnoy, on the Albert to Péronne road. Having carried out this order, it had to repel a German counter-attack during the evening.

Another warm summer afternoon for daydreaming in the shade of the trees and haystacks which stretch along the Picardy countryside. About 5 o'clock, the battalion received the order to occupy Hill 122 [4] and to keep the road clear from Péronne to the village of Maricourt. The Divisional artillery comes to take its position alongside us and some shells pass over out heads before exploding on the opposite slopes which lead down towards the Somme. In the village we find the 88th Regiment of Territorials who we are replacing and who are going into reserve.

The enemy creeps into the copses along the road, under cover of nightfall. The artillery fire is now shorter and our shells explode on the same crest of the plateau and in the streets of Maricourt. The commandant and his liaison officer are asleep at the foot of the wayside calvary at the road out of Maricourt, towards the Somme. The companies, advancing in skirmishing order, fire volleys onto the road, which is plunged into darkness. The enemy does not react, but we guess that he is very near to

*us, revealing his presence by whistles and commands shouted in
a guttural voice.*

*Suddenly, shrapnel pours down on us; under the blast, I
plunge my head into my sleeping bag, – there are some cries –
then a long groaning. The commandant has been hit behind his
ear by one of the balls from the shell. The adjutant, Dudot, who
is between the two of us, has been wounded in the chest. A
moment of anguish comes as the enemy begins to fire at point
blank range. As one runner leaves, crawling to warn Colonel de
Marcilly,[5] somewhere in a house in the village, I clumsily put a
bandage on the commandant. He has lost consciousness. Helped
by some soldiers of the 2nd Company, we hoist him painfully
onto a wheelbarrow and take him along, struggling, to the field
ambulance established at the other end of the village.*

*The way along the road, cluttered by tiles that have fallen
from the roofs of the houses, amidst the cross-fire of the infantry,
is a difficult problem to resolve. We go forward, heads lowered,
arching our backs, keeping the wheelbarrow and its burden
steady by a miracle of balance. But luck favours us and we arrive
without any new injuries at the door – a low roofed house where
the medics welcome us.*

*Colonel de Marcilly has set up his post alongside and after
receiving my report, I get the order to tell my company that it
must go immediately to Billon Farm, a huge structure,
surrounded by walls, on the road to Bray, where it will spend the
night.[6]*

As it left for Billon Farm, the 69e R.I. handed the village over to
the 45e R.I. which then held on to it, despite furious German attacks.
The main street in Maricourt even today, is named after the 45e R.I., in
honour of this defence.[7] Sergent Fourrier Garbolde continued his
narrative:

*Billon, in the night, appeared before me with its vast gate, its
yard filled with manure and its white buildings on which danced,
by the candlelight, our troubled shadows. Tomorrow, all of it will
burn and crumble under the furious wind of incendiary shells.*

The 69e R.I. re-grouped on the morning of 27 September, for the
attack on Montauban which would mainly be undertaken by the 3rd
Battalion with its 12th Company in the forefront of the assault. The
village at this stage was held by a regiment of Bavarian troops.[8] Sergent
Fourrier Garbolde continued:-

Captain Huin, with his huge moustache and big staring eyes commands us and it's in his company that the liaison officer sets off towards Hill 104.[9] It will reach Montauban by taking advantage of the ravine which separates the villages of Carnoy and Mametz.[10] The advance was easy, without any reaction from the enemy for the fog scarcely dissipated and favoured our venture.

The difficulties will begin with our arrival on the crest of Hill 136, which dominates the area.[11] Montauban appears with its red roofs that emerge through the trees and the orchards that surround it.[12] A real Picardy village, as we will come to know so many, – riddled with traps, dense hedges, barbed wire and vast barns.

The Bavarians in Montauban suddenly came under the joint fire of French '75' field artillery and accurate small arms fire from the 12th Company. They suffered immediate heavy losses at the hands of the French and began to flee towards the east, allowing the 12th Company to capture the village, taking prisoner one officer and twelve men.

For the moment there is a deadly silence. A patrol goes along the main road, the only one, along the edge of which stands the church, the town hall and the deserted dwellings. Chance

French heavy artillery in action. Note the lack of helmets and the basic protection for the gun position – all to change as the war progressed.

favours us, – the Germans have evacuated, or haven't yet occupied our objective.

The companies are placed in the shape of a fan in the orchards. One of them will occupy the tile works which raises its brown mass at the end of the Péronne road which is a dangerous position to watch over.[13] The 1st Company is installed in the orchards to the west, with the task of observing Mametz Wood which is facing it. The 2nd Company extends in line from there.

The command post is placed in a little abandoned café at the entrance to the village, in the direction of Carnoy. Colonel de Marcilly, the regimental standard, the sappers and the medics join us there which is a large group of people for such a tiny place.

The respite was short lived. At about 10 o'clock in the morning, the bombardment of the village begins. Shells of all calibres crash down around us and houses begin to catch fire. Losses are light, for apart from us, there is no-one in the houses. The companies in their orchards are spared the firing which is concentrated on the road, where it is impossible to show your face. We wait philosophically for the shell that will dislodge us from this wretched café, but the roof holds and it protects us throughout the day.

German infantryman wearing a pickelhaube.

At nightfall, the 3rd Company moved to the western edge of the village to await the inevitable German counter-attack. This eventually came from the direction of Mametz Wood and was repulsed by the French. However, this success was the only one in the area, and as the flanks either side of Montauban were still in German hands, the 69e R.I. holding the village found itself dangerously exposed. Inevitably, on the morning of the 28th following a violent bombardment and under cover of a dense fog, the Germans swept the Frenchmen from their positions and re-captured the village.

With the return of night, we have to be doubly vigilant for the guns have given way to the German infantry who are crawling towards the orchards. Completely terror stricken, a man from the 2nd Company comes to inform us that ahead of his company masses of Germans are moving around in the darkness and that the shrill noise of a fife rises from Mametz Ravine.

As I go for news, trying to keep my balance over the ruins of the houses, (for the road has disappeared under the debris), gunfire breaks out. Bullets whistle on all sides and the enemy begins to surround Montauban. My company, well sheltered behind its hedges, retaliates and the concerted firing stops the waves that climb the slopes of the Montauban ridges. Night passes with successive alerts but the regiment holds on well and the enemy begins to entrench behind small parapets of earth. The village is a vast inferno which lights up the night and one can no longer venture forth without being hit on the head by a piece of roof or wall.

Dawn is born in the fog and the cold. The shooting doubles, for there is nothing more favourable to an attack, than mist. The German artillery haphazardly bombards the exits to the village in the hope of hampering the comings and goings and the re-supplying of our troops. Our café ends up being half collapsed and we take refuge against its outside walls in a small yard near to a carpenter's workbench.

But here come the company runners who are just outside the village. They announce breathlessly and with broken voices that the enemy has infiltrated under cover of the fog and their comrades are beginning to be shot down from the ruins of the houses. There is nothing more to do but free ourselves from Montauban's trap, for it would be ridiculous to let ourselves be caught up in the mesh of the net which is being slowly but surely woven .

Despite courageous counter-attacks, the Germans could not be wrested from the village and, eventually and inevitably, the French were forced to withdraw.

Colonel Marcilly gives the order to withdraw into Carnoy. It has to be sent to the companies in the orchards. I leave as if in a dream and join my old friend from the time in the barracks at Essey, Lieutenant François, who commands the 1st Company. Words are exchanged quickly in a whisper ..... 'evacuation of Montauban' ..... 'the way to 'Carnoy' ..... 'surrounded' ..... .

The order is passed from mouth to mouth and the men get up, numb with cold and covered with dew. In single file they cross through the orchards where they tear what is left of their greatcoats on the wire and 'artificial brambles'. It will be necessary to abandon without burial, those who were the dear friends of our happy days at Nancy, fallen, their heads on the barrels of their guns, in the orchards of Montauban. Each name spoken evokes a memory, a face full of youth – but have we got time to think? Time passes and soon Montauban will be nothing but a cemetery in the hands of the enemy.

On the road to Carnoy there is congestion, despite the instructions to observe spacing out between each man. The shells that relentlessly accompany us crash down heavily on the packs of soldiers who are moving down the slope of the road. A discharge of shrapnel knocks poor François to the ground. We tend and support him as far as Carnoy where he gives his last sigh.[14] Our wounded follow, trailing behind, leaning on their guns or helped by a stick. I guide a friend who was in the next bed to me in the barracks, a tough farmer named Maitre, from the Champagne region. His body is now bloodless, his eyes already glazed, and he will stagger only to the first houses of Carnoy.

Jolival, a good sort, whose fate will soon be decided in the mud of Flanders,[15] took command from the first. With what remains of the company, he will hold on to the ruins of Carnoy where the defence is organised. We crouch beside Captain Huin in a haystack on the highest point of Carnoy and it is there that the wave of German attacks of September die. Carnoy will hold out and our battalion will affirm its qualities of resistance and fidelity to the orders it received.

French prisoners of the Germans, 1914-15.

During the course of the morning of 28 September a popular officer from the Company, Capitaine Henri Thierion de Monclin, was killed trying to hold back one of the German attacks. He and his men are commemorated just outside the village, not far from the former orchards, on the site of the old Montauban windmill.[16]

After the main fighting of September had died down, the battle lines which remained, left the Germans in command of the high ground and their enemies below them – not just on the Somme – but, by the end of the year, from Nieuport in Belgium through to Belfort on the borders of Switzerland. Having held Carnoy and Maricourt, the French front line ran to the north of these villages with the Germans firmly entrenched on top of the Montauban Ridge. The battle lines would stay that way until July 1916 and Montauban would remain firmly in German hands for the next twenty-one months.

For its part in the fighting of September 1914, the village was awarded a Croix de Guerre with palm, by an Army Order of 27 October 1920, which stated:

> 'situated in the midst of the fighting during the war it was totally destroyed by multiple bombardments and the course of bitter combat in 1914. It has always shown the greatest qualities of courage and self-denial in adversity and has richly deserved the honour.

Worse was to come than 'the course of bitter combat in 1914'.

The British

In the early summer of 1915, following a disastrous half year for the French, the British Army began taking over the northern part of the Somme sector from the French Army to alleviate some of the strain and make a firm commitment to the war on the Western Front. A new British army, the Third Army, was formed to execute this task and four divisions arrived to take over the 17 miles of land. One of these was the 18th (Eastern) Division.

The 18th (Eastern) Division

On 6 August 1914 the British Parliament had sanctioned the raising of 500,000 men to swell the ranks of the Regular Army for the duration of a war which popular opinion was convinced would be over by Christmas. One of the few people in the country to realise that this would not be the case, however, was the newly appointed Secretary of State for War, Earl Kitchener of Khartoum. On 7 August he made his famous appeal for 100,000 men, the idea being that each of the county infantry regiments of the Army would raise one battalion each, to be numbered in sequence after the Territorial Force battalions. These were to be known in the popular press as *'The First Hundred Thousand'*, or *'K1'* Divisions, the *'K'* obviously standing for Kitchener and officially, to distinguish them from the Regular Army and Territorial Force soldiers, they were to be known as New Army troops.

On 11 September 1914, Army Order 382 had authorised, amongst other things, the raising of six more Divisions of infantry for the New Army. These were the second wave of volunteers following Kitchener's second appeal for men on 28 August. As a result, they were often known as *'The Second Hundred Thousand'* or *'K2'* Divisions. The 18th (Eastern) Division began to form in September 1914 from men drawn mainly from East Anglia and the home counties. Most of its men had joined up for patriotic reasons, for *'three years, or the duration of the war'*, [17] once it was obvious that the war would most definitely not be over by Christmas. Like their predecessors in the 'K1' Divisions, this war service meant that the new battalions, raised from within the old regular county regiments, would be titled 'Service Battalions'. Their support troops, such as artillery, engineers and train, also specifically raised for war service did not have the *'Service'* in their titles, however.

After the formation of the Division, units destined for the 18th Division were given initial training – often under the most haphazard circumstances that marked the New Armies of 1914 and 1915. They all came together on Salisbury Plain in early May 1915, with Divisional headquarters being based at Codford St. Mary. On 24 June the Division was inspected by King George V and in early July received warning of its imminent move to France. Exactly one month to the day, after its royal inspection, forward elements of the Division began the move, with Divisional headquarters leaving on the following day. By the end of the month, the whole Division was in France, concentrated near Flesselles, near Doullens, initially under X Corps of the Third Army. After some of its units had undergone trench experience with the 4th and 51st Divisions, the Division took over the line from Fricourt to Mametz on 22 August 1915 to begin an association with the area and the Montauban Ridge which would last for the rest of the war. Its Divisional sign was the letters ATN, formed in a circle, which, at first sight bore no relation to its Divisional number or its main geographical area of recruiting. However, if the letters were spoken quickly, they made the sound *'eighteen'*. This unusual idea was suggested by Major General F.I. (Ivor) Maxse, commander of the Division for most of the war.

The Divisional sign of the 18th Division

The Division consisted of three infantry brigades and all the support troops needed to sustain them in the field. These infantry brigades were numbered 53, 54, and 55. In the early stages of the war it was easy to work out which brigades were in which Division – as there were three brigades to a Division, the middle brigade number was three times the Divisional number. Thus the middle brigade in the 18th Division was ɔ4 Brigade. Once the build up to the Somme battle started, however, this simple rule became a little blurred, as brigades were swapped round for operational reasons, as we shall see.

53 Brigade consisted of four infantry battalions: 8th (Service) Battalion, The Norfolk Regiment, 10th (Service) Battalion, The Essex Regiment, 6th (Service) Battalion, The Royal Berkshire Regiment and 8th (Service) Battalion, The Suffolk Regiment.

The 8/Norfolks had been raised in Norwich, Norfolk, in September 1914 from local volunteers.[18] It moved to Shorncliffe almost immediately and in October 1914, it was sent to Colchester, Essex and in April 1915 to Codford St. Mary on Salisbury Plain. The Norfolk Regiment itself was raised in 1685 and became The 9th Foot, or East Norfolk Regiment, in 1685.[19] This meant that it was the 9th infantry regiment in seniority in the British Army. At the Battle of Almanza in 1707, during the Wars of the Spanish Succession, it covered the retreat of the army, when the battle against the French was lost and prevented a total rout. As a result, it was granted the figure of Britannia as a badge, as its heroism symbolised the strength of the nation. A hundred years later, during the Peninsular War, the Spanish locals mistook this badge for a figure of the Virgin Mary and so venerated the men from Norfolk. This so amused the rest of the British troops present, that the 9th was given the nickname *'The Holy Boys'*, which still stuck to them a hundred years after that. Its regimental march, not unnaturally, was *'Rule Britannia'*.

The 10/Essex Regiment was formed at Warley, Essex in August 1914 and trained at Shorncliffe and Colchester before moving to Codford St. Mary in May 1915. Its parent regiment was formed in 1881 with the amalgamation of The 44th Foot, raised in 1741 and The 56th Foot, raised in 1755. Its cap badge was the castle of Gibraltar within a wreath, surmounted by a sphinx, which testified, amongst many other battle honours, to its presence at the siege of Gibraltar between 1779 and 1782 and in Egypt, during the 1884-5 campaign. Its nicknames were *'The Two Fours'* and *'The Little Fighting Fours'* which alluded to the numbering of the 44th Foot and *'The Pompadours'*, which alluded to the fact that they were supposed to have taken their unusual purple full dress uniform facings from the livery of Madame de Pompadour, one of Louis XIV's mistresses.

The 6/Royal Berkshires was raised at Reading, Berkshire, in September 1914 and after training at Colchester, Essex, it too, arrived at Codford St. Mary in May 1915, to prepare for overseas service. Its parent unit, officially titled Princess Charlotte of Wales's (Royal Berkshire Regiment), had originally been raised as two separate regiments, The 49th Foot, in 1743 and The 19th Foot in 1755. During the Cardwell reforms of 1881 it became officially associated with Berkshire when the two regiments were amalgamated. Its distinctive cap badge, also worn by its New Army battalions, was a Chinese dragon, awarded for service at the Taku Forts in the 2nd China War of 1860. One of its nicknames was *'The Brave Boys of Berks'*.

The 8/Suffolks was formed at Bury St. Edmunds on 9th September 1914 and first trained at Shorncliffe, then in October 1914 in Colchester, and finally in May 1915 at Codford St. Mary. It was a service battalion of the regular Suffolk Regiment which was first raised in 1661 and became The 12th (East Suffolk) Regiment of Foot, in 1782. Its cap badge was, like that of The Essex Regiment, the castle of Gibraltar, with its key, which signified that it, too, had been present at the siege of the rock from 1779 to 1793. Around the castle was the Latin motto of Gibraltar, *'Mons Insignia Calpe'*, (The Rock is the Badge of Gibraltar) and around this a wreath laurel, the whole surmounted by a royal crown, although The Suffolk Regiment was not, in fact, a Royal Regiment. Royal Regiments, which usually wore blue facings on full dress uniform (the Suffolk Regiment wore yellow), were regiments granted royal status for some particular act on behalf of the sovereign or some particularly noteworthy action in battle. The motto of the Suffolks, *'The Old Dozen'* alluded to its numerical sequence in the infantry order of battle.

54 Brigade consisted of four infantry battalions, The 11th (Service) Battalion, The Royal Fusiliers, The 6th (Service) Battalion, The Northamptonshire Regiment, The 7th (Service) Battalion, The Bedfordshire Regiment and The 12th (Service) Battalion, The Middlesex Regiment.

The 11/Royal Fusiliers was formed at Hounslow in Essex, on 6th September 1914 and first trained at Colchester, and then in May 1915 it left for Salisbury Plain, for its final home training. Its parent unit, The Royal Fusiliers, had a long and celebrated association with the City of London. In fact its full title was The Royal Fusiliers (City of London Regiment). Originally raised by King James II to protect his guns at the Tower of London, it was first named The Ordnance Regiment, before becoming The 7th Foot. As its original duty was to act as guards, its members were issued with a fusil, a superior weapon to the ordinary musket and they were the first English troops to carry them. Eventually, all fusiliers, or those who carried the fusil, wore as their badge a flaming grenade, to symbolise their other rÙle as bombers. The badge of the Royal Fusiliers became the flaming grenade with the rose of England on the body of the bomb, encircled in a garter motto with the words *'Honi soit qui mal y pense'* (Evil be to he who evil thinks).

The 6/Northamptons was formed at Northampton in September 1914 and in November was sent to Colchester, Essex, before moving to Salisbury Plain. Its parent unit, The Northamptonshire Regiment came into being in 1881, with the amalgamation of the old 48th Foot (Northamptonshire Regiment) raised in 1740 and The 58th Foot (Rutlandshire) Regiment, raised in 1755. Its regimental cap badge, like the Essex and Suffolk regiments, bore the castle of Gibraltar and its key, with the battle honours 'GIBRALTAR' above, and 'TALAVERA', below, the whole surrounded by a laurel wreath, with the regimental title at the bottom. At Talavera in 1809, during the Peninsular War, the 48th won undying fame for its conduct during the battle and its colonel, the last officer in the British Army to wear a tricorn hat, earned renown by urging his men forward by raising the hat aloft as he lay dying. This accounts for one of the regiment's nicknames – *'Heroes of Talavera'*. Another nickname was *'The Steel Backs'* gained because of the stoicism of its men undergoing the ritual and brutal punishment of flogging.

The 7/Bedfords was raised at Bedford itself in September 1914 and was first attached to Army Troops of the 15th Division at Aldershot. On 25 February 1915 it was sent to Colchester, as part of 54 Brigade, 18th Division and then to Salisbury Plain. Its parent unit in the Regular Army, the Bedfordshire Regiment was raised in 1688 as the 16th Foot and in 1782 became known as the Buckinghamshire and Leicestershire Regiment, before beginning its association with Bedfordshire in 1809. At the Battle of Walcourt in 1689, it fired the first shots ever by the British Regular Army on the Continent against the French and in the first quarter of a century of its existence, it fought more battles than any other single battalion regiment. Its cap badge bore the device of a buck or hart crossing a ford, within the garter motto, on a cross patté and starburst, with the regimental title underneath. One of its nicknames, *'The Old Bucks'*, referred to its badge and its early

Some members of the 7/Bedfords in 1915.

association with Buckinghamshire and another, *'The Featherbeds'*, was a play on words of its title and the fact that in the 18th century it went for many years without fighting a major engagement.

The 12/Middlesex Regiment was formed at Mill Hill in August 1914 and was then sent to Colchester, before being sent to Salisbury Plain. Its parent unit, The Duke of Cambridge's Own (Middlesex Regiment), came into existence in 1881, with the amalgamation of the 57th Foot, raised in 1755 and known as the West Middlesex Regiment and the 77th Foot, raised in 1787 and known as the East Middlesex Regiment. Its cap badge featured the Plume of the Prince of Wales and the cipher and coronet of The Duke of Cambridge, who had been a former colonel, a wreath of laurel, the regimental title and the battle honour 'ALBUHERA'. This bloody battle, in the Iberian Peninsula in 1811, was especially hard fought by the 57th Foot, whose colonel at the time was mortally wounded and as he lay dying, he asked to be propped up, and rallied the Middlesex men with the cry *'Die hard, my men, die hard.'* Ever after that day, the regiment was known as *'The Die-hards'.*

55 Brigade also consisted of four infantry battalions; 7th (Service) Battalion, The Queens (Royal West Surrey Regiment), 8th (Service) Battalion, The East Surrey Regiment, 7th (Service) Battalion, The Buffs, (East Kent Regiment) The 7th (Service) Battalion, The Queen's Own (Royal West Kent Regiment).

The 7/Queens was formed at Guildford, in September 1914 and was then sent to Purfleet, Essex. In April 1915 it left for Colchester, Essex and was then posted to Salisbury Plain. Its parent regiment, The Queens (Royal West Surrey Regiment), was the second infantry regiment in seniority in the British Army, having been raised in 1661 by the Earl of Peterborough. The Earl had been given the job of governing the north African town of Tangier, which was part of the dowry of King Charles II's consort, Catherine of Braganza. The regiment was first known as The Tangier Regiment and then The Queen's, in honour of Catherine. Its cap badge was a Paschal Lamb (the lamb slain and eaten at the feast of the Passover), and flag, which was part of the arms of the Royal House of Braganza. Most of the nicknames associated with the regiment, *'The Lambs', Kirke's Lambs',* and *'The Mutton Lancers'* were allusions to this badge, although 'The Tangerines' obviously came from its first tour of duty.

The 8/East Surreys was raised at Kingston-on-Thames in September 1914 and also trained at Purfleet in Essex. In April 1915 it left for Colchester and then in May was despatched to Salisbury Plain. Its parent regiment, The East Surrey Regiment, was formed in 1881 by an amalgamation of The 31st Foot and The 70th Foot. The 31st had originally been raised as a marine unit in 1702 and took part in the capture of Gibraltar and later fought at Dettingen in 1743, where George II led the Army – he was the last British monarch to go into battle. After the battle, King George saw the light coloured facings of the 31st and mistook them for The Buffs. When this mistake was pointed out to him, he called out *'Well done, then, Young Buffs.'* As a

Men of the Queen's Regiment whilst in training in 1915.

result, *'The Young Buffs'* became one of the regiment's nicknames. The 70th Foot was originally raised as a second battalion of the 31st Foot and became a separate unit in 1756. It became known as The Surrey Regiment in 1825, when it first formed its association with the county. The cap badge of the parent unit featured part of the arms of Kingston-on-Thames on an eight pointed star, with the regimental title below and the royal crown above.

The 7/Buffs, was formed at Canterbury, Kent, in September 1914 and, like the 8th East Surreys, was first sent to Purfleet, then Colchester and then Salisbury Plain. Its parent regiment The Buffs (East Kent Regiment), was originally raised in 1572 by the citizens of London, to aid the Protestant cause in Holland and its members were largely local volunteers from the old City of London Train Bands. Known at first as The Holland Regiment, it was retitled The 3rd Foot in 1665 and had to exchange its buff leather jackets for the scarlet tunics of English Infantry of the Line. In recognition of its former service, however, it was allowed to retain buff uniform facings and, certainly by 1702, was better known as The Buffs. Its association with the County of Kent began in 1782 when the title East Kent Regiment was conferred upon it. Its cap badge, the Welsh dragon, was part of the arms of the royal house of Tudor and this was shown standing over the regimental title.

The 7/Royal West Kents was formed at Maidstone on 5th September 1914 and also trained at Purfleet, Colchester and Salisbury Plain. Its parent regiment, officially titled The Queen's Own (Royal West Kent Regiment) was an amalgamation, once more as a result of Cardwell's Army reforms in 1881, of the 50th Foot and the 97th Foot. The 50th was originally raised in 1756 as the 52nd Foot, but was re-titled two years later. It began its associations with west Kent in 1782 and won its royal title in 1830. The 97th Foot was originally raised in 1824 as The Earl of Ulster's Regiment, and it was often known as *'The Celestials'*, on account of its sky blue facings. Other nicknames associated with the West Kents were *'The Dirty Half Hundred'* gained after the battle of Vimiera in 1808 on the Peninsula, when The 50th Foot routed the French, blackened with gunpowder and grime and *'The Blind Half Hundred'*, gained purportedly because at one time, the whole regiment was stricken with eye trouble. Its cap badge was the white horse of the County of Kent, with the Latin motto *'Invicta'*, (Unbeaten) in gothic characters surmounting the regimental title.

The Pioneer Battalion for the 18th Division was The 8th (Service) Battalion, The Royal Sussex Regiment. It was raised as an infantry

ERECTED
TO THE MEMORY OF
PRIVATE A. E. LAWTON
179th COMPANY ARMY SERVICE CORPS
18th DIVISION SUPPLY COLUMN
BRITISH EXPEDITIONARY FORCE
BY THE
OFFICERS N.C.O's AND
MEN OF HIS COMPANY

This stone memorial was recently discovered buried under rubble near the railway station in Albert. MZ/032814 Private Alfred Lawton from Birkenhead, Cheshire, died on 4 August 1915 and is buried in Terlincthun British Cemetery, Boulogne. It is probable that Pte Lawton was the first member of the unit to die on active service.

battalion at Chichester, west Sussex, in September 1914 from where it was posted to Colchester. It became Pioneer Battalion to the 18th Division on 4th February 1915, and three months later went to Salisbury Plain to join the rest of the Division. Its parent regiment had been raised in 1881 with an amalgamation of The 35th Foot and The 107th Foot. The 35th Foot had been raised in 1701 and most of its early years was spent as marines. In remembrance of this, its officers always drank the Loyal Toast seated, in common with the Royal Navy, as the low decks in the wooden ships of the line did not permit them to stand. It first became associated with Sussex in 1804 and was granted the royal title 28 years later. The 107th Foot was originally raised in India as the 2nd Bengal European Infantry and only received its numerical title in the British Army infantry order of battle in 1854, when it arrived in England. Its cap badge was the Star of the Order of the Garter, with the regimental title below and a plume of feathers above. This plume, know as the Roussillon Plume, was gained for service at the Battle of Quebec under General Wolfe in 1759, when the 35th Foot routed the French Roussillon Grenadiers and captured its colours, which displayed the devices of the Roussillon Plume and a golden fleur-de-lys. The soldiers of the regiment actually wore a plume in their caps until 1810 and were nicknamed *'The Orange Lilies'* because of the golden fleur-de-lys and the fact that they had worn orange facings until being granted royal status in 1832. After this time, the regimental facings became blue.

Apart from the 8/Royal Sussex Regiment, the 18th Division was served by all the ancillary units necessary for any Division in the line. Many of these were initially given the number '18' to identify them with their parent Division, but as with infantry brigades, as the war progressed and transfers for all sorts of military reasons were made in and out of the Division, the numbers did not always tally. As well as infantry and pioneers, the 18th Division was served by mounted troops, field artillery, trench mortar batteries and ammunition columns, engineers, signals, medical, veterinary and sanitary troops and train troops - made up from the Army Service Corps.

When the 18th Division was formed, its mounted troops were found by the 18th Divisional Cyclist Company, raised in December 1914, before the realities of trench warfare were to make cycle-mounted troops of limited use on the Western Front. In June 1916, just before the Division's departure for France, the cyclists were joined by C Squadron of the Westmorland and Cumberland Yeomanry and although this regiment crossed the Channel as part of the Division, it left it before the start of the Somme battle, as did the cyclists.

Artillery was based on brigades, initially of six batteries per brigade, but after February 1915, four batteries per brigade. Each of these batteries contained four guns. The 18th Divisional Artillery consisted of LXXXII to LXXXV Brigades – numbered in Roman numerals to distinguish them from batteries, which were numbered in Arabic numerals. These brigades were served by Brigade Ammunition Columns at first, but in May 1916, with the experience that war brought, these were abolished and integrated into the already constituted 18th Divisional Ammunition Column. Up until June 1916 the Division did not possess its own trench mortar batteries, as these were also organised on a brigade level, but after June 1916 it was able to call on X18, Y18 and Z18 Medium Trench Mortar Batteries and V18 and W18 Heavy Trench Mortar Batteries. Initially, also, it had the 18th Heavy Battery Royal Garrison Artillery of 60 pounder howitzers allocated to it, but when the Division left for France this battery stayed behind and fought for the rest of the war in the Middle East and Salonika and thus was never on active service with the Division.

Before the Division left for France it had been allocated the 79th 80th and 92nd Field Companies of the Royal Engineers and the 18th Divisonal Signal Company and these units remained with it for the rest of the war, as did the 30th Mobile Veterinary Section, the 18th Divisional Train, consisting of the 150th, 151st 152nd, 153rd and 179th Companies of the Army Service Corps. The 35th Sanitary Section also joined the Division in England and served with it throughout the Somme battle until March 1917.

Medical support for the 18th Division was provided by 54th 55th and 56th Field Ambulances of the Royal Army Medical Corps, all three of which joined the Division on 18th June 1915 and stayed with it for the remainder of the war.

The 30th Division

Officers' pattern 30th Divisional Patch, hand embroidered white thread on black cloth mounted on khaki uniform cloth. In 1916 the patch was sometimes worn below the collar on the back of the tunic.

The 30th Division first came into being as the 37th Division on 10 December 1914, with the authorisation of the raising of a Fifth New Army – i.e. the fifth hundred thousand volunteers needed for war service. The six new Divisions which made up the Army were to be numbered 37th to 42nd. However, in April 1915, the original Fourth New Army was broken up to replace expected casualties in the first three New Armies and as the Fifth New Army then took over the title of Fourth New Army, its six Divisions were re-numbered 30th to 35th. In point of fact, however, although most of the battalions which would make up the 30th Division were unadopted by the War Office, until May 1915, they had commenced their military training in September 1914.

Throughout August 1914 recruiting figures in Britain remained high. These did not even dip significantly when the news of losses began to emerge from Belgium and France following the Battles of Mons and Le Cateau. No stretch of media propaganda could disguise what was obviously happening on the Continent, but far from dulling the public's enthusiasm to enlist, the realisation of what lay ahead seemed to bring the best ideals of patriotism and duty to the fore.

In the main the new recruits were from the agricultural, unemployed, unskilled or semi-skilled classes of society – the traditional areas of recruitment in peacetime. However, Lord Kitchener soon came up with the idea, intuitively correct, as it turned out, that there was still an untapped source of new recruits who had not yet thought of joining the colours – the educated middle classes who ran the offices and business houses on which the country's prosperity was based. Kitchener realised that there was no lack of patriotic fervour amongst these people, it was just that they had not realised that they were needed and had assumed that they were better placed keeping the wheels of the country's businesses turning smoothly.

On 24 August he first mentioned his ideas to the 17th Earl of Derby, of Knowsley, near Liverpool, who had already earned himself the unofficial title *'England's Best Recruiting Sergeant'* for the work he had done for recruitment in the north-west of England. Derby was of the opinion that he might be able to raise a battalion of men (roughly a thousand in number), from the business houses of Liverpool and sought and gained Kitchener's permission to try. Consequently, on 27 August 1914, he announced in the Liverpool press his intention of raising a battalion of comrades who worked and enjoyed leisure time together, to serve their King and Country together - and invited all those interested to meet the following evening.

It so happened that Kitchener chose the following day, 28 August, to make his appeal for his *'Second Hundred Thousand'* and perhaps because of this extra piece of encouragement, far from getting his anticipated 1,000 men, Derby discovered well over double that number waiting to hear him speak. In his patriotic and rousing speech, the earl first suggested the title by which the Liverpudlians and many more men all over the north of England would be known in the future – Pals. Within six weeks he had enough volunteers from Liverpool to fill four complete battalions of men, eventually to be known as the 17th to 20th Battalions of The King's (Liverpool Regiment), with two more incomplete reserve battalions to recruit and 'feed' the first four. In recognition of his having been personally responsible for raising what amounted to a brigade of infantry, King George V later granted the right of these *'Liverpool Pals'* to wear the crest of the Derby family as a cap badge, rather than the prancing White Horse of Hanover, worn by most of the other battalions of the King's. Moreover, so proud was Derby of his men that he gave each of the first recruits a solid silver version of their cap badge.

That was not all, however. At the same time that Derby was raising his Pals battalions in Liverpool, at his suggestion, the Mayor of Manchester, Alderman Sir William McCabe, was calling upon the young men of Manchester to make a similar gesture. The response was also similar, with four thousand Mancunians enlisting almost immediately and a further four thousand within three months. They would become the 16th to 23rd Battalions of The Manchester Regiment. Thus, by the end of the year, there were eight battalions of Manchester Pals and four of Liverpool Pals under training, and many others Pals battalions from different towns raised and being raised throughout the north.

Lord Derby, who had had a long political interest in Manchester, was similarly delighted with the Mancunian response and he wished them, also, to wear his crest as a cap badge. It is said, however, that Kitchener vetoed the idea on the grounds that with over 12,000 men all wearing the Derby device and as yet unadopted by the War Office, they would become the biggest 'private' army in the country. Consequently, the Manchester Pals wore the arms of the City of Manchester throughout their existence. In deference to Lord Derby, however, the 30th Divisional sign was a version of his crest, similar to the cap badge of the Liverpool Pals but without the family motto underneath. Nevertheless, whatever badge either wore, the Liverpool and Manchester Pals *were* in essence a 'private' army until the late spring of 1915, when they were officially adopted by the War Office. Up until that time they were funded, billeted and organised by Lord Derby and the councils and people of the two great cities of the industrial north west.

Throughout the winter of 1914-1915 the battalions which made up what would become the 30th Division trained and equipped in their own localities, the Liverpool battalions in local parks and eventually on the estate of Lord Derby at Knowsley and the Manchester battalions in Heaton Park, Manchester. At the end of April 1915 the battalions began to entrain for Belton Park, in Grantham, Lincolnshire, the seat of Lord Brownlow, and they were gradually joined there over the next four months by their support forces. In September 1915 the whole Division, now officially renamed the 30th Division, moved for its final pre-France training to Salisbury Plain in Wiltshire, before beginning the embarkation process from Folkestone and Southampton on 6 November. After concentrating all the troops at Ailly le Haut Clocher north west of Amiens, the Division entrained for its destiny on the Somme and XIII Corps. At this time, its infantry consisted of 89, 90 and 91 Brigades.

In early December it was decided to swap one brigade from the New Army's 30th Division with one from the Regular Army's 7th Division. The logic behind the swap was that 'amateur' New Army Divisions would need some 'stiffening' if they were to face a resolute and largely professional German enemy on the Somme. As the events of 1 July 1916 turned out, this move would not have been necessary, but the calibre of the New Army troops had not been tested in battle at this stage. Accordingly, 91 Brigade was chosen for the swap and on 19 December left for the 7th Division. In return, the 30th Division received 21 Brigade, made up from Regular Army infantrymen who were the second battalions of famous county regiments. Further to this line of action, within the 30th Division itself, on 21 December 1915, the 19/Manchesters of 90 Brigade was swapped with the 2/Royal Scots Fusiliers and joined 21 Brigade and on Christmas Day 1915, the 18/King's of 89 Brigade was swapped with the 2/Bedfords and also joined 21 Brigade. By these expedients, all the brigades of the Division

Men of the Manchester Pals at Grantham in 1915.

had Regular Army 'stiffeners' for the coming battle. By this time, all infantry troops from the Division had been given their first 'baptism of fire' by being attached to experienced troops in the line at the northern edge of the Somme front near Hébuterne. Thus, on New Year's Day 1916, the 30th Division infantry consisted of three infantry brigades, 21, 89 and 90.

21 Brigade had four infantry battalions, 18th (Service) Battalion, (2nd City), The King's (Liverpool Regiment), 2nd Battalion, The Duke of Edinburgh's (Wiltshire Regiment), 19th (Service) Battalion, The Manchester Regiment, (4th City) and 2nd Battalion, Alexandra, Princess of Wales's Own (Yorkshire Regiment).

The 18/King's was raised by Lord Derby on 29 August 1914 as the second of the Liverpool 'City' Battalions. It underwent its preliminary training at the Hooton Park Racecourse on the Wirral side of the River Mersey, before moving into Knowsley Park before Christmas. On 30 April 1915 it went to Belton Park, Lincolnshire before being posted to Larkhill Camp on Salisbury Plain, for final training before embarkation for France. As we have already seen, in common with all four battalions of The Liverpool Pals, it wore the Derby crest as a cap badge. This consisted of an eagle perched on a cradle, over a cap of maintenance, above the Derby family motto, *'Sans Changer'* (without change). The origins of the eagle and child crest are obscure, but go back to mediaeval times, and an early branch of the Stanley family, (the family name of the Earls of Derby), the Lathoms, when a baby was

Men of the Liverpool Pals under training in 1915.

15520 Pte J R Owen 17 KLR wounded at Montauban 1 July 1916, he survived the war.

discovered in the grass below an eagle's eyrie and subsequently accepted as an heir.

The Liverpool Pals' parent regiment, The King's (Liverpool Regiment) had been raised in 1685 as Princess Anne of Denmark's Regiment. For its illustrious service during Marlborough's campaigns in the Low Countries in the early years of the 18th century, Queen Anne re-named it The Queen's Regiment and it became The King's Regiment on the accession to the throne of George I in 1715. In 1751, it became the 8th Foot and was first officially linked to the city of Liverpool in 1881. Its regimental march was 'Here's to the Maiden of Bashful Fifteen', which was parodied by the Pals with a version they sang to the words 'Why Did We Join the Infantry ..... We must have been Bloody Well Barmy'

The 2/Wiltshire Regiment was a Regular Army Battalion, first raised in 1824 as The 99th (Lanarkshire) Foot and became associated with the Duke of Edinburgh some years afterwards. On the outbreak of war it was serving as a garrison battalion at Gibraltar and on 31 August 1914 it sailed for Great Britain, arriving at Southampton on 3 September, after which it joined 21 Brigade, 7th Division, at Lyndhurst, Kent. On 7 October 1914 it landed at Zeebrugge, Belgium and took part in the First Battle of Ypres. It was then in action at Langemark, Gheluvelt, Neuve Chapelle, Aubers Ridge, Festubert, Givenchy and Loos, before joining the 30th Division on the Somme. Its parent battalion, the 1/Wiltshires, had been raised in 1756 and was given the title the 62nd Foot, two years later. Its association with the county of Wiltshire began in 1782. Among it nicknames were 'The Splashers' and 'The Moonrakers'. The former alluded to a distinction gained after the Battle of Carrickfergus Castle in 1760 when, in an action against the French, having run out of ammunition, the men used up their tunic buttons before resorting to bricks and stones. In commemoration of this action, before the universal button with the Royal Arms was issued to them with the introduction of the khaki uniform, they wore tunic buttons with a dent or 'splash' in them. They were called *'The Moonrakers'* because apparently one night whilst members of the regiment were on anti-smuggling duties, they were surprised dragging a pond with rakes in an attempt to recover some smuggled kegs of brandy. When asked what they were doing, some of the soldiers replied that they were looking for the moon. The cap badge of the Wiltshire Regiment was a cross pattée with a ducal coronet on top, the cipher and coronet of The Duke of Edinburgh in the centre and the regimental title on a scroll below.

The 19/Manchesters had been raised by the Lord Mayor of Manchester, Alderman Sir William McCabe on 28 August 1914, as the fourth of the Manchester City Battalions. It first trained at Heaton Park, Manchester before going to Belton Park, Grantham, in April 1915 and Larkhill Camp, Salisbury Plain, in September 1915. Its parent regiment, The Manchester Regiment was created in 1881 as an amalgamation of the 63rd Foot and the 96th Foot. It had started its service to the crown as the second battalion of the 8th Foot, in 1756 becoming a separate regiment, the 63rd Foot, two years later. The 96th Foot was raised in 1824 and inherited the traditions of a former regiment of that number, disbanded in 1818. The cap badge of The Manchester Regiment was the arms of the City of Manchester, although at the Battle of Guadeloupe in 1759 it had won the right to wear the fleur-de-lys, having defeated French soldiers who wore that device. Although a fleur-de-lys badge was worn by the 7th Battalion, of the Territorial Force, the rest of the regiment did not actually wear this as a badge until 1930, as the documents authorising its wearing had been mislaid.

The 2/Battalion, Alexandra, Princess of Wales's Own (Yorkshire Regiment), better know as The Yorkshire Regiment or The Green Howards was a Regular Army battalion, and on the outbreak of war was stationed at Guernsey, in the Channel Islands. It returned to England on 28 August 1914 after which it joined 21 Brigade, 7th Division at Lyndhurst, Kent. On 6 October 1914, it landed at Zeebrugge, Belgium and took part in the First Battle of Ypres. It then fought at Langemark, Gheluvelt, Neuve Chapelle, Aubers Ridge, Festubert, Givenchy and Loos. On 20 December it joined the 30th Division on the Somme at Fienvillers. Its parent battalion had been raised in 1688 as Luttrell's Foot and it became the 19th Foot not long afterwards at about the same time it began its association with the

North Riding of Yorkshire. In 1875 it became Princess of Wales's Own and in 1901, Alexandra Princess of Wales's Own Yorkshire Regiment. The title Green Howards, by which it was always more popularly known, however, came about because at the same time that The Buffs had a commander named Howard, so did the Yorkshire Regiment. The Yorkshire commander then changed the regiment's facing to the colour green, and it became known as Howard's Greens and eventually The Green Howards, to distinguish it from The Buff Howards. The regimental cap badge had been personally designed by Queen Alexandra when she was the Princess of Wales. It consisted of her personal cipher interlaced with a Danish cross, the Dannebrog, illustrating her origins, and the date 1875, which was when she first became associated with the regiment. This was shown over the regimental title and a Yorkshire rose, and the whole was surmounted by a princess's coronet.

89 Brigade consisted of four infantry battalions, 17th (Service) Battalion, (1st City), The King's (Liverpool Regiment), 19th (Service) Battalion, The King's (Liverpool Regiment), (3rd City), 20th (Service) Battalion, The King's (Liverpool Regiment), (4th City) and 2nd Battalion, The Bedfordshire Regiment.

The 17/King's was the first of the Liverpool Pals to be raised, as the 1st City or Commercial Battalion, on 29 August 1914. It moved almost immediately into the old premises of the Prescot Watch Factory near the Derby estate and then to Knowsley Park. On 30 April 1915 it went to Belton Park and in September to Larkhill Camp on Salisbury Plain, before leaving for France in November 1915.

The 19/King's was formed on the same day as the 17th as the 3rd City or Commercial Battalion and, as there was no training camp available for its recruits, they had to drill in a Liverpool Park each day and go home at night, until November 1914 when the Knowsley Park camp, built on Lord Derby's estate, became available. After this, its training history in England was the same as the 17th Battalion's

The 20/King's was the last of the four Liverpool Pals battalions to be formed, to complete a brigade of Liverpool Commercial or City recruited infantrymen. It was raised at Liverpool on 16 October 1914 by Lord Derby and first went to Tournament Hall, Knotty Ash to train and then to Knowsley Park. After this, its training history was the same as the 17th and 19th Battalions.

The 2/Bedfords was a Regular Army battalion and was stationed at Roberts Heights, Pretoria, South Africa, on the outbreak of war. It returned to England in September, landing at Southampton on 19

September 1914 after which it joined 21 Brigade, 7th Division at Lyndhurst, Kent. On 7 October 1914, it landed at Zeebrugge, Belgium and took part in the First Battle of Ypres. It then fought at the Battles of Langemark, Gheluvelt, Neuve Chapelle, Aubers Ridge, Festubert, Givenchy and Loos. On 19 December 1915, 21 Brigade joined the 30th Division on the Somme after which the Battalion was swapped with the 18th King's and joined 89 Brigade.

90 Brigade consisted of four infantry battalions, The 2nd Battalion, The Royal Scots Fusiliers, The 16th (Service) Battalion, The Manchester Regiment (1st City), The 17th (Service) Battalion, The Manchester Regiment (2nd City) and The 18th (Service) Battalion, The Manchester Regiment (3rd City)

The 2/Royal Scots Fusiliers was a Regular Army battalion, performing garrison duties in Gibraltar on the outbreak of war. In September it left for England and joined 21 Brigade, 7th Division at Lyndhurst, Kent. On 6 October 1914, it landed at Zeebrugge, Belgium and took part in the First Battle of Ypres and then fought at Langemark, Gheluvelt, Neuve Chapelle, Aubers Ridge, Festubert, Givenchy and Loos. On 19 December 1915, 21 Brigade was swapped for 91 Brigade and joined the 30th Division on the Somme and then the Battalion was swapped with the 19/Manchesters and joined 90 Brigade. The parent battalion of The Royal Scots Fusiliers was raised in 1678, the oldest fusilier regiment and the second oldest Scottish regiment in the British Army. Originally titled The Earl of Mar's Fusiliers, after its founder, Charles Erskine, Earl of Mar, it was renamed The 21st Foot, ten years later. Erskine had issued the regiment with fusils, which was remembered on its cap badge, a flaming fusilier grenade with the Royal Arms on the body of the bomb. The regiment's nickname, *'Earl of Mar's Greybreeks',* also alluded to the colour of its trousers when first raised. It is probable that The Royal Scots Fusiliers was the last infantry regiment to carry its colours into battle, during The Zulu War.

The 16/Manchesters was formed at Manchester on 28 August 1914 by the Mayor of Manchester, Alderman Sir William McCabe, the first of the Manchester City or Manchester Pals battalions. Its initial training was at Heaton Park, Manchester and in April 1915, it went to Belton Park, Grantham and in September to Larkhill Camp, on Salisbury Plain. before leaving for France in early November.

The 17/ and 18/Manchesters were the 2nd and 3rd Manchester City battalions and like the 16th Battalion, were raised on 28 August 1914 by the Lord Mayor of Manchester. Their training histories were also the same as the first Manchester City Battalion and like this battalion, they too left for France in early November 1915, landing at Boulogne.

The pioneer battalion for the 30th Division was The 11th (Service) Battalion, The Prince of Wales's Volunteers (South Lancashire Regiment). The Battalion was raised by Lord Derby at St. Helens, Lancashire on 1 September 1914 as an infantry unit, and in February 1915 was sent to Bangor, Caernarvonshire. Some time after that it changed its role to a pioneer battalion and on 14th May 1915, it joined the 30th Division at Grantham, Lincolnshire as Divisional Pioneers. It was posted to Larkhill and Salisbury Plain, in September and it landed at Le Havre, on 7 November 1915. It was always known as The St. Helens Pioneers. Its parent regiment came into being in 1881 with the amalgamation of the 40th Foot and the 82nd Foot. The 40th Foot was raised in 1717 in Nova Scotia - the first infantry regiment to be raised after the accession of the House of Hanover to the British throne. It was first titled Philipp's Regiment and received its numbering in the infantry line sequence in 1751. The 82nd Foot was raised in 1793 and its first colonel was a member of the royal household of the Prince of Wales, later to be King George IV. At the start of the French Revolutionary Wars, the regiment volunteered, as a man, for active service and then in 1801 for service in Egypt. So impressed with these two gestures was the Prince of Wales, that he honoured the regiment with the title 'Prince of Wales Volunteers'. It then fought alongside the 40th Foot under General Abercromby against Napoleon at the Battle of the Nile in 1801. Consequently, when a cap badge was needed for the new regiment in 1881, it was not difficult to pick the Egyptian sphinx, surmounted by the Prince of Wales's feathers, the whole surrounded by a wreath of laurel, with the regimental title above and below. The regiment was often known by the nicknames 'Fighting 40th' and 'The Excellers', both based on its number in the infantry order of battle, the second from the Roman numerals, for 40, 'XL'.

Like the 18th Division, the 30th was served by all the ancillary units necessary for any Division in the line. Many of these were also initially given the number 30 to identify them with the Division, but as with the infantry brigades, as the war progressed the numbers did not always tally. As well as infantry and pioneers, the 30th Division was also served by mounted troops, field artillery, trench mortar batteries and ammunition columns, engineers, signals, medical, veterinary and sanitary troops and train troops.

When the 30th Division was formed, its mounted troops were found from the 1/Lancashire Hussars and the 30th Divisional Cyclist

Company, raised in September 1915, before the realities of trench warfare were to make cycle-mounted troops of limited use on the Western Front. Both left the Division in France in May 1916.

The four artillery batteries raised to support each of the three infantry brigades of the 30th Division were CXLVIII, to CLI Royal Field Artillery Brigades, all designated *'County Palatine'* – as they had been raised by Lord Derby within the County Palatinate of Lancashire. A County Palatine was the area or province presided over by a feudal lord. In fact, CXLIX Brigade was later commanded by The Hon. G.F. Stanley, one of Lord Derby's brothers, and two other members of the family also served the guns of the County Palatine Artillery. These brigades joined the Division at Grantham in August 1915.

They were also served by Brigade Ammunition Columns at first, but in May 1916, these were abolished and integrated into the already constituted 30th (County Palatine) Divisional Ammunition Column. Light trench mortar batteries and machine-gun companies were organised on a brigade footing once the Division arrived in France and up until June 1916, there were no divisional trench mortar batteries. However, in April 1915 X30, Y30 and Z30 Medium Trench Mortar Batteries joined the Division.[20]

From the time the Division was at Grantham, it had been allocated the 200th, 201st and 202nd (County Palatine) Field Companies of the Royal Engineers and the 30th Divisonal (County Palatine) Signal Company and these units remained with it for the rest of the war as did the 40th Mobile Veterinary Section and the 70th Sanitary Section. The 30th Divisional Train, consisting of the 186th, 187th 188th and 189th Companies of the Army Service Corps joined the Division on its arrival in France in November 1915.

Medical support for the Division was provided by 96th, 97th and 98th (County Palatine) Field Ambulances of the Royal Army Medical Corps, which joined the Division on 2nd November 1915, just prior to its embarkation for France. They then stayed with it until the end of the war.

The Task

The reasoning and strategy behind the July attack on the Somme has been covered extensively elsewhere and needs no refreshing here, but it is important to understand how much the topography of the area around Montauban would affect the attacking lines of XIII Corps, under the command of Lieutenant-General W. N. Congreve, V.C., on that momentous day.

The front line manned by the corps extended from just west of Carnoy to Maricourt where it butted onto the French XX Corps [21] – the right of line, in fact, of the whole British Army on the Western Front. For the most part, it looked up the slope of the Montauban Ridge to the German lines on the top. The German defences consisted of three main positions. The first position was the front line which was situated below Montauban and the ridge itself, just where the ground started to

rise up to the ridge. Behind this was a reserve line, between 700 and 1,000 yards back, dug not long before the expected attack and consisting of Pommiers Trench,[22] which connected with Train Alley[23] which in turn connected with Alt Trench. The eastern end of Alt Alley, at this point named Favière Alley, was in the territory to be attacked by the French. Running around Montauban itself was a long communication trench named Montauban Alley which stretched from the outskirts of Mametz village to the eastern end of Montauban. Beyond this was a long valley, aptly named Caterpillar Valley, because of its shape and some 3,000 yards further back was the German second main

These very rare photographs showing 27502 Pte A R Woods 18/KLR, on the Somme in early 1916. He was killed in action on 1 July at Montauban.

Germans in what is thought to be Montauban Alley in 1915.

position on the upper slope of Caterpillar Valley, which ran from Bazentin le Petit, in front of the two Bazentin woods past Bazentin le Grand and Longueval through Guillemont to Maurepas. The German third main position was not fully constructed by the beginning of July.

The front and reserve lines were further defended by a series of fortifications and strongpoints or redoubts, so constructed with trench blocks, barbed wire and machine-gun positions that they offered all round defence and could hold out if the main trenches were breached. These were Pommiers Redoubt, just behind Pommiers Trench, The Castle, actually behind the front line position known as Mine Trench, The Loop, at the eastern end of Pommiers Trench and Glatz Redoubt which began at what was the junction of Train Alley and Alt Trench. Dublin Trench led out of Glatz Redoubt to a further fortified position, known as The Dublin Redoubt which was in the territory to be attacked by the French. Montauban itself was also heavily fortified (the once characteristic red roofs of the houses long since destroyed) and the ruined buildings prepared for defence. The village itself was further defended by a position named Southern Trench by the British, which ran all around its western and southern perimeter.

The plan for the capture and holding of Montauban Ridge was divided into three distinct phases. The first phase, scheduled for the first day, was to begin with the capture of the German reserve line, Pommiers Trench through to Dublin Trench, to link up with the French. This would then allow the attackers to move forward and capture Montauban itself. Once the village and the top of the ridge had fallen, the left flank of the attack was to move forward to take the second objective, Montauban Alley, to gain a foothold on the immediate downward slope of Caterpillar Valley. The second and third phases, which depended on the success of the first day's fighting, would involve moving through Bernafay and Trônes Wood to the German second position at Guillemont, with the French taking Hardecourt and Maurepas.

The 18th Division's left flank was in touch with the 7th Division of XVth Corps, east of Mametz. It was to move forward with its three infantry brigades in line, from left to right, 54, 53 and 55, up two spurs of land, the Mametz Spur and the Carnoy Spur, either side of Carnoy Valley. Its initial objectives were the German reserve line of Pommiers Trench to Train Alley. After this had fallen, the advance was to continue, with the brigades still in line, through Pommiers Redoubt and The Loop to the Mametz to Montauban road and through to Montauban Alley. If this advance was successful, (quite a feat, as it would involve crossing nearly 2,000 yards of the most hostile ground), the Division was to push forward on its left flank to capture a projecting portion of the Mametz Spur which pushed into Caterpillar Valley and would allow excellent observation into the valley and beyond. The 18th Division was commanded by Major-General F.I. Maxse, who had assumed command on 2 October 1914 and would hold the appointment until January 1917.

The 30th Division had its left flank against the 18th Division on the left side of Talus Boisé, and its right flank up against the French 39th Division of XX Corps. On its left flank, 21 Brigade was to move forward and take the eastern portion of Train Alley and then move onward to take and hold Glatz Redoubt. 89 Brigade, meanwhile, was to push forward through Germans Wood and take Casement Trench, which ran westwards from Dublin Redoubt and hold it until the French had taken Dublin Redoubt and the advance was able to continue up the slope towards Montauban itself. Meanwhile, the third brigade of the Division, 90 Brigade, was to pass through the newly captured positions and take Montauban. At this time. the 30th Division was commanded by Major-General J.S.M. Shea, who had taken over command on 17 May 1916.

Both Divisional assaults were to be covered by 'creeping barrages' which would follow a set timetable and move from one objective to the next, in six 'lifts' as each position was taken. It can easily be imagined, consequently, how important it was in these circumstances that each objective fell on time.

In corps reserve, ready to exploit any major breakthrough, was the 9th (Scottish) Division, under the command of Major-General W.T. Furse. It was positioned near Billon Wood, two miles to the rear, sheltered from view and shellfire by the crest of Maricourt Ridge.

The scene was set.

The Germans

Up on the high ground around Montauban awaiting the inevitable British assault by the 18th and 30th Divisions was the German 12th Division, with elements of the 10th Bavarian Division and some of the 28th Reserve Division.

Reserve troops in the German Army were a little like the British Territorial Force except that, with compulsory conscription in Germany for all fit men over the age of twenty years, the number of trained reserve troops available for the war machine was vastly higher. In peace time each man was required to serve for at least two years in the army, or for three years in élite regiments such as horse artillery or cavalry, as the kudos accrued by serving in these units made the extra service worthwhile once a soldier had returned to civilian life. After this, he was transferred to the Reserve until the age of 26 and had to return twice a year for periods of up to eight weeks each to retrain and maintain military skills.

Thus, although there were no semi-permanent, part-time units in the German Army like the British Territorial Force, units of the Reserve, which were affiliated to regular army units, did contain troops who had served together for two years and then would come together again twice every year for the following six years. Not only were they probably better trained that the British Territorials, but there were a lot more of them. Once German Reservists reached the age of 26, they

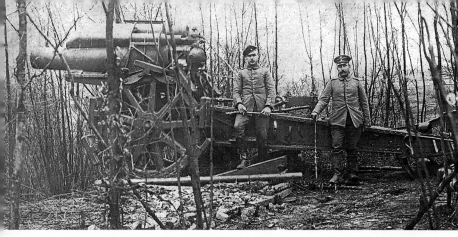

German Foot Artillery on the Somme.

transferred to the Landwehr, or second line reserves, and then at the age of 37, to the Landsturm, which was little more than military registration in peace time, but after this they continued to train with the same comrades, until they were 45 years old. Thus, there was no equivalent of the military novices of the British Kitchener Battalions in the German Army, as on the outbreak of war at least, all fit men up to the age of 45 years of age would have undergone a strict regime of military training and service for some 25 years.

By July 1916 a typical German infantry Division, regular or reserve, consisted of one brigade of infantry, made up of three infantry

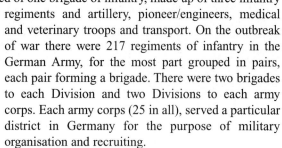

regiments and artillery, pioneer/engineers, medical and veterinary troops and transport. On the outbreak of war there were 217 regiments of infantry in the German Army, for the most part grouped in pairs, each pair forming a brigade. There were two brigades to each Division and two Divisions to each army corps. Each army corps (25 in all), served a particular district in Germany for the purpose of military organisation and recruiting.

In the summer of 1915, however, 63 Divisions lost one each of its four regiments and these were used to raise 21 new Divisions. This meant that the original 63 Divisions were reduced to three infantry regiments each, which were then re-formed into a single brigade. After the losses of Verdun and the Somme, the remaining German Army Divisions which still retained four infantry regiments, also lost them, to form yet more infantry Divisions. However, by the

German Reserve infantryman on the Somme, 1916.

time the fighting started on the Somme, a German infantry regiment consisted of three battalions, each of which was slightly smaller than its British Army counterpart and thus a German infantry Division consisted of nine infantry battalions, as opposed to twelve British – and the overall numerical strength was therefore considerably less.

Each infantry regiment in the German Army bore a title based on a number of possibilities. These were: its state, or area of origin, (and its local seniority within that state or area), its élite status, if it had one, (i.e. Fusilier-Regiment, Grenadier-Regiment, etc.), its association with a famous soldier or noble person and its regimental number in the German Army Order of Battle. Thus, Grenadier-Regiment, Kronprinz (1. Ostpreussisches) Nr. 1, or The Crown Prince's First East Prussian Grenadier Regiment No. 1, was an élite regiment, not only because it bore the name of the son of the Kaiser, but was also designated a grenadier regiment, rather than just an infantry one. It was also the first

German photographs of Montauban in early 1915.

German Officers' Mess in the village of Montauban during the winter of 1915/16.

infantry regiment in the line, from the state of East Prussia and its seniority made it regiment No. 1 in the German Army Order of Battle. In peacetime, there were 182 regiments in the numerical Order of Battle, plus units of the Prussian Guard and further units of the Bavarian Army. Bavarian regiments in the German Army always had their regimental number first, to distinguish them from the rest of the army, as Bavaria was semi-autonomous in the German armed forces – e.g. 6. Infanterie-Regiment, Kaiser Wilhelm, König von Preussen, or Kaiser William of Prussia's 6th Bavarian Infantry Regiment. In shortenend form, the letter 'J' was often used instead of 'I' to represent 'Infanterie', so that it was not confused with the numeral '1'. Thus the abbreviated form for the above regiment was 6. B.J.R..

Although the German 28th Reserve Division held some parts of the front opposite the troops of XIII Corps, most of its men faced the British 7th Division north of Mametz. However, on the evening of 30th June 1916 the line from Mametz to the Carnoy to Montauban road was held by Reserve Infanterie-Regiment Nr. 109, which formed part of the German 55th Brigade. Directly opposite the British 54 and 53 Brigades, and with its headquarters company in Pommiers Redoubt, was a battalion of troops from this unit. It should have been relieved in the line on the night of 30th June/1st July, by J.R.23, but although $1\frac{1}{2}$ companies of this regiment got through the bombardment to the front line, it is doubtful if any of the 109th actually got away. Its parent unit in the regular army was 1. Badisches Leib-Grenadier-Regiment Nr. 109, or 1st Baden Bodyguard Grenadier Regiment No. 109, and its men came from Karlsrühe in the state of Baden, which was part of XIV Armeekorps, also based at Karlsrühe. Baden was a Grand Duchy within the German Empire and its troops wore the insignia of the state, a griffin, on the front of their pickelhauben, or spiked helmets.

Reserve Infanterie-Regiment Nr. 109 fought in the Great War almost from its start and left Emmendingen, in Baden, for the front on 10 August. It was in action on the River Vosges against the French by the end of that month and then went down to the River Meurthe in early September, where it incurred serious losses. After this mauling, it retired towards Blamont and entrained at Teterchen in Lorraine for the Somme and arrived at Cambrai on 26 September as part of the 2nd Army. Throughout 1915 it stayed on the Somme, mainly across the Albert to Bapaume road from Ovillers to Fricourt. It was generally the policy of the German Army to station its troops in one area and keep them there, so that they would understand the territory and reap the benefits of knowing the topography of the land very well. Certainly after the start of the battle at Verdun, it did not have the manpower to move troops around the front anyway. The British, on the other hand tended to rotate troops from one area to another to give them more flexibility – especially as the Army expanded in size before the Somme battle.

The German 12th Division was a regular army Division from Upper Silesia and belonged to Armeekorps VI, which had its headquarters at Breslau. By July 1916, it had three infantry regiments in the line, J.R. 23, J.R. 62 and J.R. 63, all of which belonged to the German 24th Infantry Brigade. Infanterie-Regiment von Winterfeldt, (2. Oberschlesisches) Nr. 23, or von Winterfeldt's 2nd Upper Silesian Infantry Regiment No.23, came from Neisse; 3. Oberschlesisches Infanterie-Regiment Nr. 62, or the 3rd Upper Silesian Infantry Regiment No. 62 came from Cosel and Ratibor; and 4. Oberschlesisches Infanterie-Regiment Nr. 63, or the 4th Upper Silesian Infantry Regiment No. 62, came from Oppenheim and Lublinitz.

This photograph, taken from the German position at Montauban a few weeks before the attack, shows the hedgerows that were to shelter German snipers and bombers on July 1st.

The photograph above shows Bernafay Wood in October 1915. The German dugout pictured left was in the northern corner of the wood. Taken before the Somme battle began, it shows the extensive nature of a deep German dugout.

The 24th German Infantry Brigade, as part of the 12th Division, 5th Army, under Kronprinz Wilhelm, had its first engagement on 22 August 1914 at Rossignol les Bulles and having passed the Meuse, fought the battles of Laheycourt and Villette on 7 September. Following the German reversals on the Marne, it was engaged in the Champagne area, at Berru and Nogent l'Abbesse, near Reims, on 21 September, and then remained on the Reims front until mid June 1915. Then it was relieved from Champagne and transferred to the Artois region, where it occupied a sector south of Souchez, and was engaged in some very heavy fighting in the first half of July. After a brief rest and refit near Cambrai it arrived on the Somme front for the first time in October 1915 and first faced the British Army in the line near Contalmaison. On the eve of the Battle of the Somme it was still in that area.

Two battalions of J.R. 23 were in support behind Montauban and in Caterpillar Valley and it should have relieved R.J.R.. 109 on the evening of 30 June/1 July but because of the bombardment, only 1½

The photograph right, shows the same dugout captured after the offensive in 1916.

companies actually got through, the rest remaining in Montauban. All three battalions of J.R. 62 were in support from Montauban, including the Briqueterie, down to Hardecourt and all three battalions of J.R. 63 were facing the French *'Corps de Fer',* also in support from Hardecourt down to the River Somme at Curlu.

Although not part of the German 12th Division, the German regiment that faced the greatest part of XIII Corps' onslaught was 6. Bayerisches Reserve Infanterie-Regiment. It had been placed at the disposal of the Division from the 10th Bavarian Division, which was part of III Bayerisches Armeekorps, based at Nürnberg. Its regular parent regiment was 6. Infanterie-Regiment, Kaiser Wilhelm, Kônig von Preussen, whose depot was at Amberg, east of Nürnberg. It had first seen active service at

Tournai in Belgium in April 1915, after which it was sent to the Somme. There, it took over the sector covering the Lihons-Estrée road to Foucaucourt and remained there until mid June, when it began to transfer to the defensive line in front of Montauban. There, its sector of trenches stretched from the Carnoy to Montauban road in front of the British, right across to the River Somme, in front of the French. All three battalions were in position in time for the assault of the 1 July and it is probable that many of the troops had been in the front line for less than twenty-four hours when the attack began, braving the allied bombardment to get there.

Not fully in the line and taking no real part in the battle of 1 of July were men of the 12th Reserve Division which was also part of Armeekorps VI, with its base at Breslau in Silesia. It had been formed upon the outbreak of war and had fought with distinction in the Meuse-Argonne area in 1914, in Champagne in 1915 and at Verdun in 1916, where it lost 71% of its infantry troops. It consisted of the 22nd and 6th Reserve Infantry Brigades made up from R.J.R. 23, R.J.R. 38, R.J.R. 51 and Reserve Jäger Bataillon Nr. 6. Jäger troops were the equivalent of the British light infantry regiments and had originally being lightly equipped for rapid deployment and skirmishing. Before the war each Armeekorps had one battalion of Jägers numbered in Armeekorps sequence.

The 12th Reserve Division had arrived at Cambrai in early June for a rest from almost continual service in the front line and was in the process of being brought up to Montauban and Hardecourt, when it was obvious that a British and French attack was imminent. It would not arrive in the area in full strength until 2 July, however, by which time it was too late to alter the outcome of Congreve's XIII Corps' attack.

Thus was the scene set for the most decisive battle ever fought around the little Picardy village.

A portable notice board, in a German trench at Montauban in early 1916 which displays maps of German successes on the Eastern front.

The Stationmaster's house at Mountauban: before the war, during the German occupation; and today (rebuilt).

Notes

1 Historique du 69e Régiment d'Infanterie, published in 1928.

2 Commandant Joseph Ducrot died of wounds in a field hospital at Amiens on 11 October 1914.

3 This wood was later called La Guerre Wood on British maps, but it was untitled then, as now, on French maps.

4 Hills on French Army maps were always named after the spot height in metres above sea level, even though they might not have been of appreciable size, unlike, say, Hill 60, near Ypres. There are a number of high points measuring around 120 to 124 metres in this area, but Sergent Garbolde is probably referring to the high ground on the Albert to Péronne road – the modern D 938.

5 Lieutenant-Colonel Petitjean de Marcilly died of wounds received in action, at a field ambulance at Hem, on 1 November 1914.

6 Billon Farm still stands today, although rebuilt since the Great War.

7 See Chapter Three

8 These men were almost certainly from the 4th Bavarian Division. As such, they would have belonged to the 5th or 9th Bavarian Infantry Regiment of the 7th Bavarian Brigade or the 5th or 8th Bavarian Reserve Infantry Regiment of the 5th Bavarian Reserve Brigade.

9 This is no more than a spot height just north of the Mametz to Carnoy road.

10 This is Carnoy Valley and not really large enough to be called a ravine in 1914 or today.

11 This must be the ridge upon which Montauban stands.

12 Before the Great War the eastern side of Montauban was full of orchards, none of which remain today. Even by 1916, the only evidence of them on British Army maps was Orchard Copse, a small wooded area about 300 yards on the right hand side of the road to Mametz.

13 Sergent Fourrier Garbolde is confusing a 'tuilerie' or tile works with what was in fact a 'briqueterie' or brick works, which stood on the right hand side of the Maricourt to Montauban road, south of Bernafay Wood, which later figured in the fighting of 1 July 1916.

14 In fact, Sous-Lieutenant Edmond François did not 'give his last sigh' at Carnoy on 28 September 1914, but died of his wounds in a Paris hospital on 1 October.

15 Sous-Lieutenant Jean-Désiré Jolival died of wounds at Furnes on 30 November 1914.

16 See Chapter Four - The Monclin Memorial.

17 These were the time schedules under which soldiers enlisted.

18 Most of the early service battalion movements in England are taken from British Regiments 1914-1918, by Brigadier James. See the bibliography for further details.'

19 Most of the references to individual regimental histories are taken from The British Army, by Talbot-Booth. See the bibliography for further details.

20 V30 Heavy Trench Mortar Battery joined the Division towards the end of the Somme battle, in October 1916.

21 The French XX Corps had had vast experience at Verdun, which was to be of great value once the attack started and had earned itself the title 'Corps de Fer' or The Iron Corps.

22 This was so called because of the apple orchard that had been on the main road before the war.

23 This was named after the remains of the Albert to Péronne light railway line which snaked through XIII Corps' attack area.

ORDER OF BATTLE OF THE 18TH AND 30TH DIVISIONS ON THE SOMME 1 JULY 1916

XIII CORPS (Lieut-Gen. W.N. Congreve V.C.)

18th (EASTERN) DIVISION (Maj. Gen. F.I. Maxse)

53 Brigade
8/Norfolk Regiment
6/Royal Berkshire Regiment

10/Essex Regiment
8/Suffolk Regiment

54 Brigade
11/Royal Fusiliers
7/Bedfordsire Regiment

6/Northamptonshire Regiment
12/Middlesex Regiment

55 Brigade
7/Queen's
7/Buffs

8/East Surreys Regiment
7/Royal West Kent Regiment

Pioneers
8/Royal Sussex Regiment

30th DIVISION (Maj. Gen. J.S.M. Shea)

---

21 Brigade
18/King's Liverpool Regiment
(2nd Pals)
19/Manchester Regiment
(4th Pals)

2/Wiltshire Regiment

2/Green Howards

89 Brigade
17/King's Liverpool Regiment
(1st Pals)
19/King's Liverpool Regiment
(3rd Pals)

20/King's Liverpool Regiment
(4th Pals)
2/Bedfordshire Regiment

90 Brigade
2/Royal Scots Fusiliers
16/Manchester Regiment (1st Pals)

17/Manchester Regiment (2nd Pals)
18/Manchester Regiment (3rd Pals)

Pioneers
11/South Lancashire Regiment

Chapter Two

THE BATTLE

Just before 7.30 am on 1 July 1916, sheltering in their front line and assembly trenches and hearing the constant scream of shells passing overhead on their way to the German lines, the men of XIII Corps, apprehensive, like any troops awaiting battle, nevertheless had every reason to feel optimistic. They were all volunteers – they had either joined the Regular Army in pre-war post-Victorian certainty, or the New Army in indignant determination to right a hideous wrong, after the German invasion of Belgium – and they had a belief in their officers and staff as yet unsullied by the casualties and failures to come.

The very bombardment that deafened them gave then total confidence in their coming success, for they could not believe that anyone or anything could survive its ferocity. Originally scheduled to last five days, bad weather had meant a postponement of the attack for forty-eight hours and the consequent lengthening of the bombardment, which consequently lasted for a whole week. At this point, the allied artillery was much more numerous than that of the Germans. Thus there was one heavy gun or heavy howitzer for every forty-seven yards

A heavy Howitzer in readiness to bombard the German lines.

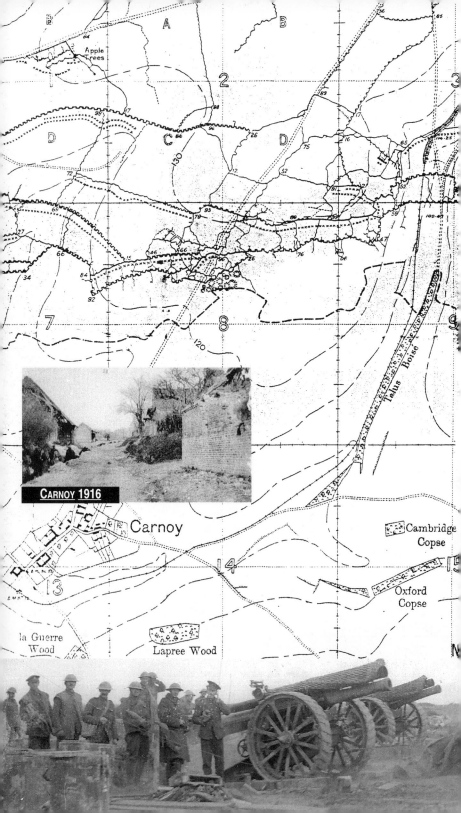

B

A

B

Apple Trees

2

3

D

C

D

7

8

9

Talus Boisé

CARNOY 1916

Carnoy

Cambridge Copse

13

14

15

Oxford Copse

la Guerre Wood

Lapree Wood

N

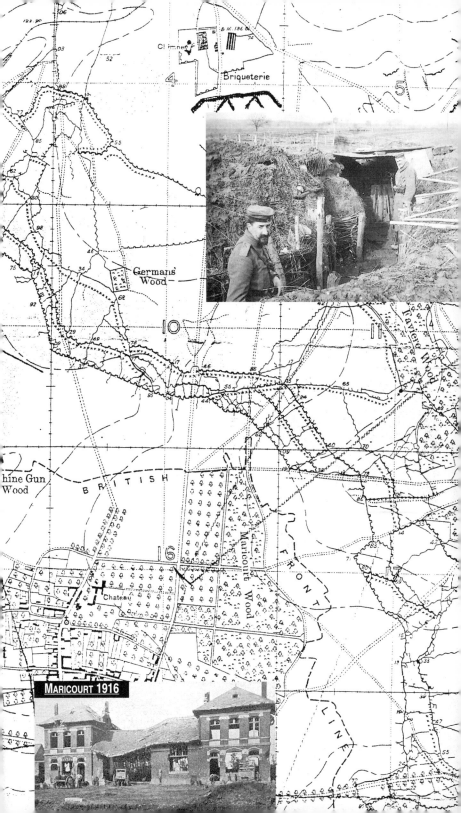

Briqueterie

Germans Wood

Taviers Wood

hine Gun Wood

BRITISH

FRONT LINE

Maricourt Wood

Chateau

MARICOURT 1916

of front and one field gun or light howitzer for every seventeen yards.[1] Once the barrage lifted from the front line German trenches, all the infantry had to do was to get out into the open, cross No Man's Land at a fairly leisurely pace and take charge of the German trenches, where there would be no serious opposition. At least that was what they believed.

The German counter-bombardment – for at last the Germans knew where and when the attack would take place – did not begin in earnest until 26 June, but throughout the night of 30 June/1 July there was very little German shelling of XIII Corps' positions, except for some 5.9 inch howitzer activity on Carnoy. It was not heavy enough to hamper the progress of troops moving forward into their assembly positions, however. Meanwhile, along the XIII Corps front, 'Russian Saps', tunnels with small charges laid at their ends, had been excavated by the 183rd Tunnelling Company of the Royal Engineers across No Man's Land, in some cases to within twenty yards of the German front line.

At exactly 6.25 am the intensity of the British bombardment increased to hurricane proportions, with the German lines still shrouded in mist. Dawn on that day was actually about 4.30 am, but an attack time of 7.30 am was decided upon to give better observation for an attack which depended on artillery – and also because the French had virtually insisted on it. At 7.00 am the mist began to clear along

Men unloading a supply of shells for the bombardment.

the whole front and, shortly afterwards, the ends of the Russian Saps were blown open. At 7.22 Stokes Mortar batteries, firing from the ends of these saps, began to drop rounds on the German front line at a rate of thirty per minute. Eight minutes later, when the barrage began to shift to previously registered points in the German defensive system, whistles blew along the long line of the allied assault and the greatest adventure in the history of warfare began.

Captain, (later Lieutenant Colonel) Neil Fraser-Tytler of CLI (County Palatine) Brigade, Royal Field Artillery,[2] described the build up to this assault.

All night long the bombardment had continued, but at 6.25 a.m. the final intense bombardment started. Until 7.15 a.m. observation was practically impossible owing to the eddies of mist, rising smoke, flashes of bursting shells, and all one could see was the blurred outline of some miles of what appeared to be volcanoes in eruption. At 7.20 a.m. rows of steel helmets and the glitter of bayonets were to be seen all along the front line.

At 7.25 a.m., the scaling ladders having been placed in position, a steady stream of men flowed over the parapet, and waited in the tall grass till all were there and then formed up; at

7.30 a.m. the flag fell and they were off, the mist lifting just enough to show the long line of divisions attacking: on our right the 39th French Division; in front of us our 30th Division; on our left the 18th.

The 54 Brigade Attack

54 Brigade, under the command of Brigadier-General T.H. Shoubridge, was on the western edge of the 18th Division assault with the 11/Royal Fusiliers on the left, the 7/Bedfords on the right, the 6/Northamptons in support and the 12/Middlesex in reserve.

As the Fusiliers and Bedfords advanced across No Man's Land they found, as elsewhere along the Corps' front, that at first, anyway, artillery fire was light, probably because of the excellent counter-battery fire of the British artillery in the days before the attack, but immediately they came under heavy machine-gun fire. They discovered, however, that the German wire was for the most part destroyed, largely because of the divisional trench mortar batteries used for this very purpose. As a result, they were able to cross the German front line, named Austrian Trench at this point, without much incident. They had also been helped there by the exploding of two 500lb mines just in front of the trench, at 7.27 am, which temporarily confused the enemy. They soon began to fan forward, leaving 'mopper-uppers' to take care of the dug-outs and were then able to move forward through Austrian Junction to Emden Trench until a single machine-gun, firing from a fortified position known as The Triangle

German machine gunners await the advancing soldiers.

A Lewis gun team.

caused the leading companies of the 7/Bedfords serious losses, before they were able to storm the position and move on. All of the officers in its leading two companies were wounded or killed during this engagement and the attack was carried forward by NCOs and men.

Meanwhile the 11/Royal Fusiliers had advanced so rapidly up the Mametz Spur that they had to halt in front of the German reserve line at Pommiers Trench, to wait for the British artillery barrage to move on. By 8 am, the barrage having moved on, they were able to take the trench, with the help of the 10/Essex Regiment of 53 Brigade, and as they crossed over it, their fortunes began to change.

Ahead of them was Pommiers Redoubt, (known to the Germans as Jamin Werk), and as they came under machine-gun fire from this fortified position they were amazed to find belts of barbed wire in front of them, which had hitherto been hidden by the long grass which covered the slopes up to the stronghold. As the 11/Royal Fusiliers sent wave after wave of men forward, they were mown down by the accurate machine-gun fire. However, the redoubt jutted out from the main Mametz to Montauban road and was thus capable of being outflanked. Eventually a party of bombers and soldiers with two Lewis guns, led by Captain Johnson of the Fusiliers, entered Maple Trench from the left and managed to get round the back of it, where they were temporarily held up by snipers firing from Beetle Alley. Lieutenant W.H. Savage (who had already been wounded in the foot at 7.30) and some of his men were able to rush Beetle Alley however, and clear these snipers out. This allowed the Fusiliers to enfilade the German defenders, and burst into the redoubt itself. The Lewis gunners also made short work of some Germans who were fleeing from Fritz

65

Trench, which butted onto Maple Trench. They had been dislodged by a Stokes Mortar team which had pounded their position in that trench. Lieutenant Savage was unfortunately killed not long after this by a sniper whom he and his men must have missed. [3]

By this time the main bulk of the Fusiliers, together with men of the 7/Bedfords and some of the 10/Essex, were able to swarm into the redoubt from its eastern flank through gaps in the barbed wire. Despite a brave and desperate defence by the Germans (who were from Reserve Infanterie-Regiment Nr. 109) which lasted for the better part of an hour and saw the most vicious hand-to-hand fighting, the outcome was inevitable. Before long those Germans who were not already dead or wounded began to surrender as the remnants of their comrades began to flee across Caterpillar Valley towards the comparative safety of their own second position.

By 9.30 am Pommiers Redoubt was in British hands and the Fusiliers and Bedfords, together with elements of the 6/Northamptons, who had come up through the redoubt, pushed on across the main road to occupy Beetle Alley. This trench had fallen by 10.15 am, despite the fact that the troops on either flank of 54 Brigade's attack were still well behind. At first no further progress was made because of heavy German resistance, and the fact that the flanks were in the air, but by the early afternoon, as the German position became untenable, the men of 54 Brigade had advanced, in platoon strength at least, to occupy White Trench, on the forward slope of Caterpillar Valley. This gain, which represented an advance of some 2,000 yards, was one of the furthermost made anywhere on the day and had fulfilled all the brigade's objectives for the day.

The commanding officer of the 6/Northamptons, Lieutenant Colonel G.E. Ripley later wrote of his unit's part in the battle, to the local newspaper: [4]

To The Editor, 'Northampton Independent'
                                July 5
Dear Sir,

I shall not be disclosing military secrets if I write to let you know that the Regiment I have the honour to command went through their first big battle on July 1st. The Division to which we belong were [sic] the first, I believe, to accomplish the task allotted to them .... Personally I am more than proud of my men. They advanced through a heavy barrage of artillery fire as steady as if on parade, and straight to their allotted objectives, where they worked like Trojans amidst a heavy bombardment.

Our losses, considering what they came through, were not heavy – I am grieved that I cannot possibly write to all relations of those who have fallen on the field of honour. As it is, I have to use a Bosche telegraph form to write to you, but I ask them to accept this assurance of my deep sympathy. Their dear ones have died like heroes and not in vain.

I believe two other county regiments are fighting somewhere near us, and I trust Providence has been equally good to them. My only regret is that I am not twenty years younger - I am too old to command such splendid lads, and I feel quite ashamed to have to be helped over obstacles that others take in their stride. However, I could not be helped along better if I were their father, and like many another broken-winded old hunter, I still hope to be in at the finish.

Yours faithfully,
G. RIPLEY.

The support battalion, the 12/Middlesex took no part in the actual assault but nevertheless played its part in the action, as described in the history of the Regiment.[5]

At Zero hour (7.30 a.m.), while the assaulting troops were going forward to the attack, the 12th Middlesex were kept in the dug-outs at Carnoy. At 8.30 p.m. [sic] Colonel Maxwell moved up to the Battalion Headquarters at Piccadilly in the old British front line. At 12.45 the Middlesex moved up into the forming-up trenches, shortly afterwards crossing No Man's Land to the old German front line ..... The enemy's barrage was still falling, but it was weak and not very accurate. On Companies taking up the positions they began consolidating. The hostile trenches were much damaged and in some places almost obliterated. Dead Germans were everywhere, and some prisoners taken from dug-outs were obviously much shaken and almost incoherent. At this period one officer – 2 Lieut.. R.H. Hudlestone[6] – had been killed, two other officers wounded, three other ranks killed, 27 wounded and four missing. Throughout the remainder of 1st and during the daylight hours of the 2 July, the 12th Middlesex remained in the same positions, but at 8.30 p.m. on the latter date, the Battalion was ordered to relieve the 11th Royal Fusiliers in the advanced trenches.

The 53 Brigade Attack

53 Brigade, under the command of Brigadier-General H.W. Higginson, was in the centre of the 18th Division assault with the 6/Royal Berkshires on the left, the 8/Norfolks on the right, the 10/Essex in support and the 8/Suffolks in reserve.

The attack of the Berkshires, which would include two platoons from the 10/Essex Regiment, was potentially the most difficult within the Brigade area as it included a position known as Casino Point, where the German line jutted out into No Man's Land. The Germans had realised that this was a potentially weak spot in their line, as it could be enfiladed quite easily and, consequently, they had fortified it with a heavy machine-gun post. However, the already mentioned 183rd Tunnelling Company of the Royal Engineers had successfully tunnelled underneath it to lay a charge of 5,000 lbs. of ammonal and it was hoped that the explosion of this mine would nullify the problem.

At 7.27, as the other smaller mines in the area were detonated,[7] the Royal Engineer officer in front of Casino Point, waiting to detonate the mine, was horrified to see British infantry beginning to leave their forwards trenches and set off across No Man's Land. This put him into an obvious quandary which was soon resolved for him when he saw the machine-gun in the German position begin to fire at the advancing British and he pressed the plunger.

Lance Corporal E.J. Fisher of the 10/Essex Regiment later described what he saw from No Man's Land.

> *I looked left to see if my men were keeping a straight line. I saw a sight I shall never forget. A giant fountain, rising from our line of men, about 100 yards from me. Still on the move I stared at this, not realising what it was. It rose, a great column nearly as high as Nelson's Column, then slowly toppled over. Before I could think, I saw huge slabs of earth and chalk thudding down, some with flames attached, onto the troops as they advanced.* [8]

Captain Rochfort of the 6/Royal Berkshires was also a witness to the blowing of the mine and its effects:

> *The machine guns at Casino Point were doing quite a bit of damage when suddenly there was a*

A destroyed German stonghold.

> *blinding flash; the whole of the earth seemed to shake and the mine went up.*
>
> *The air was filled with large lumps of earth, Germans, machine-guns, baulks of wood, concrete emplacements and all the debris of the strong point itself. The crater was forty feet deep and quite thirty yards across.'* [9]

Although Casino Point was most effectively dealt with and machine-gun, machine-gunners and other defenders were blown sky high, some of the debris also hit and wounded the attacking British. The Adjutant of the 10/Essex, Lieutenant R.A. Chell, later wrote:

> *Kasino Point* [sic] *filled the air around us with lumps of chalk of varying sizes, and a fair number of our men were injured by them. Our little shack was on the trench level and was quite open on the west side. Several hunks came into this den, and the colonel's servant, Hodges, who was standing at the opening, was almost stunned. He suffered badly from concussion for the rest of the day.* [10]

However, this was a small price to pay for the relative ease of the success it gave the attackers.

As a consequence, the Berkshires were able to cross what remained of the German front line – from Austrian Trench it became Bay Trench, just in front of the Berkshires attack line, and then Mine Trench at Casino Point. The men then moved forward crossing Bund Trench and Bund Support Trench, and gained their first objective, the eastern end of Pommiers Trench, by 7.50 am. It was here that the first serious resistance of the day was encountered as German machine-guns and snipers now began to open up enfilading fire from the attackers right flank from a fortified position known as The Loop. Part of the reason for this was that the 8/Norfolks had not been able to advance so quickly and as a result, the flank was exposed. Eventually, however, by protecting this flank with bombers and Lewis gunners and receiving a company of reinforcements from the 10/Essex, they were able to hold on until the Norfolks were able to consolidate Pommiers Trench, having taken The Loop. With the fall of Pommiers Redoubt to 54 Brigade, the Berkshires and Essex were then able to push forward again to their second objective, Montauban Alley.

Crossing the Mametz to Montauban road at about mid-day, the Battalion had managed to occupy half of its allotted portion of the trench. Now supported by the 10/Essex, it slowly advanced more by short rushes and bombing forays supported by Stokes Mortar teams, rather than by an all out assault, when it came under accurate fire from a particularly determined and highly skilled German sniper. Attempts to bomb him out of his position failed and when Lieutenant F.G. Rushton of the 53rd Trench Mortar Battery moved forward to attempt to shoot him with his revolver, the sniper instead killed him with relative ease.[11] Despite witnessing this action, Second Lieutenant L.H. Saye of the Battalion then moved forward with a rifle to try and locate him, but he was also shot.[12] At this stage the Battalion's Company Sergeant Major, F.A. Sayer, decided that he would attempt to locate the sniper.

By the simple but reckless expedient of jumping onto the trench parapet, he was able to see the sniper, who immediately fired at him. At the same instant, Sayer also fired, killing the sniper with his only shot. The sniper had also hit him, however, and although severely wounded, he was eventually to recover to receive a well earned Distinguished Conduct Medal.

German sniper, with his spotter, ready to pick off the advancing soldiers.

Following Sayer's distinguished action, and further bombardment by trench mortars, Montauban Alley was finally cleared by 4.45 pm as the Germans fled across Caterpillar Valley. By the early evening, the Alley was secured and the men from Berkshire began to take stock of their incredible 2,500 yard advance.

As the Casino Point mine was spiralling its debris into the sky, the forward companies of the 8/Norfolks, with two platoons from the 10/Essex, were already advancing across No Man's Land. Helped by the firing of a flame thrower, (a Livens Flame Projector), firing from the end of a Russian Sap, which cleared the Germans from the western edge of the Carnoy Craters, they were able to cross the German front line without serious opposition. As they moved towards the German support line at Bund Support Trench, however, they came under enfilading fire from a fortified position known as The Castle, and also from Back Trench, behind Breslau Support Trench, on their right. They were able to overcome the Germans in The Castle with relative ease, but those Germans in Back Trench, which was in the area of the 55 Brigade attack, were not so easy to dislodge as they were firing from some 400 yards away. As a consequence, the advance was held up and no immediate support could be given to the 6/Royal Berkshires on the Norfolks' left.

Each time that the Norfolks tried to advance they were met with withering fire from their right, but nevertheless moved relentlessly forward, D and C Companies losing all but two subalterns between them. At about 10.30 am, they reached their first objective, and part of the eastern edge of Pommiers Trench fell to them, but they were still held up by intense machine-gun fire from The Loop, which was ahead of them and to the right. By this time Back Trench had fallen to the 55 Brigade, and with the arrival of reinforcements from B Company and a determined effort by both infantrymen and battalion bombers, The Loop was eventually taken. Its capture then allowed the Norfolks to flood down the rest of the occupied portion of Pommiers Trench and take that too.

Private F.L. Campling of the 8/Norfolks later related his part in the capture in a letter home to his native Norwich. [13]

> *Corporal Goulder glanced to right and left, and gave the word to advance, having observed our left flank making headway. Rising to my feet I saw Hotblack collapse with a bullet in the foot, and Goulder a few yards ahead shot through the head.[14] Getting down at full length, partially concealed by the vegetation, I got slowly forward and came across Sergeant Lewis*

Colman and a few of his men similarly held up. Peeping out cautiously, we observed that our bombers had gained a footing in the German fourth line trench, and were working their way up to the position of the machine gun which was causing the discomfiture of our little band.

After taking a few shots at the machine gunner, we crept, in single file to the left, entered the trench and were delighted to see the survivors of our company. We had now reached our first objective and awaiting orders to proceed, had time for a hearty handshake and a comparison of notes. At the point where the machine gun had caused our delay, a considerable number of Germans were still holding out, but our men had secured a foothold on both flanks, and the passing of the whole fourth line into our hands was only a question of time.

The final objective of Montauban Alley now beckoned, but as the Norfolk men, with the remnants of the two platoons of the 10/Essex Regiment, began to move north up Loop Trench they came under heavy machine-gun fire from the Alley and from Montauban itself. Second Lieutenant J.H. Attenborough and Regimental Sergeant Major J. Coe [15] were both killed after repeated attempts to force a way through until, eventually, Second Lieutenant E. Gundry-White with a party of bombers managed to force his way through from Loop Trench and Montauban Alley fell. This put the Battalion in touch with the 6/Royal Berkshires on its left and the 7/Queens, of 55 Brigade, on its right and made the occupation of Montauban Alley complete. Before nightfall the position was further consolidated and fighting patrols were sent out along Caterpillar and East Trenches and into Caterpillar Wood itself.

As we have already seen, although nominally in support in the attack, the 10/Essex Regiment played its full part in the fighting. Apart from the four platoons which were attached to the leading assault battalions of 53 Brigade, by the late afternoon the rest of the Battalion had been sent up the line as reinforcements, providing much needed fresh help to exhausted comrades and significantly contributing to the victories of the day.

As elements of D Company helped the 6/Royal Berkshires to take Montauban Alley, one of its officers, Captain Banks came across a small mongrel dog, presumably a former German pet:

I patted him and a Boche machine-gun opened fire, hitting the dog in the leg. We bound the little fellow up, left him in the trench, and went on. [16]

By the evening of 1 July, all four companies were quartered in captured

German trenches. The previously mentioned Lieutenant Chell, described the situation in one of these:

> At 5 p.m., Bird [17] had found a huge Boche dug-out in Mine Alley for our new Battalion headquarters. As we were still in support we might have stayed in our old position, but we all wanted to be up and residing in territory so recently Hun. This was one of the great thrills of this day. What a satisfaction it was to drag out all the German uniforms and filth from the old dug-out and set fire to it. Later, when we had dinner, (about 11 p.m., I think) we had excellent Hun sparkling water with our whisky. Everyone had endless chocolate. ..... Battalion H.Q. was reasonably comfortable, but not clean in the soldiers' sense of the word, (I caught the first louse I ever saw there). I felt so concerned that the enemy might counter-attack that I sat up all night.'[10]

The 8/Suffolk Regiment, in Brigade reserve, did not take an active part in the struggles of the day, but nevertheless contributed to the victory by carrying up ammunition, war material and water to the fighting battalions of both 53 and 55 Brigades, for which it later received a congratulatory message from Brigadier-General Sir T.D. Jackson, commanding 55 Brigade. One 8/Suffolks officer later wrote home about his experiences on the evening of 1 July:

> At about six o'clock I received orders to take a fatigue party up to Montauban with water. War in its most terrible form was now to come before my eyes. We marched over the craters and the first line of German trenches, now nothing less than ploughed

Water supplies behind the front line; water was much in demand and had to be guarded.

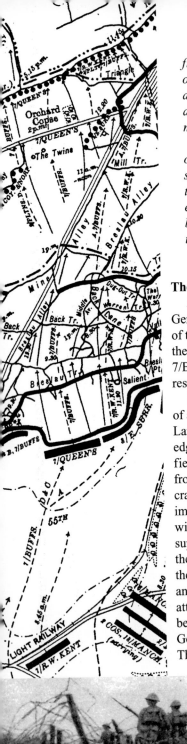

*fields. Here we got into a trench and found
our way up to the village of Montauban. I
did what I could for some of the wounded,
and those beyond human aid I gave
morphia.*

*At the top of the avenue we had to cross
over the open and dump the water-cans in a
small wood beside the road. The firing at
this point was terrific. We went over in
extended order at the double. Our going
back was even worse. We were shelled all
the way.*[18]

The 55 Brigade Attack

55 Brigade, under the command of Brigadier-
General Sir T.D. Jackson, was on the eastern edge
of the 18th Division assault, with the 7/Queens on
the left, the 8/East Surreys on the right, the
7/Buffs in support and the 7/Royal West Kents in
reserve.

Potentially its attack line was the most difficult
of all the 18th Division, as the nature of No Man's
Land in front of it varied so much. At its western
edge it was virtually non existant and a crater
field, of about 150 yards length, separated the
front lines, where a succession of mine and shell
craters overlapped to the extent that the land was
impassable. Because of this the Germans had
wired the area, before withdrawing to their
support line at Bund Support Trench, although
they still maintained some of the craters, which
they had fortified with earthworks, machine-guns
and snipers. In contrast, the centre of the Brigade
attack line was quite wide, some 250 yards
between the British front line and that of the
Germans, known as Breslau Trench at this point.
The eastern edge was, however, the most difficult

terrain. The British front line trenches at this point veered up and forward, following the contour of the land, to form a salient which jutted upwards beyond the tip of Talus Boisé. The Brigade start line was on one piece of high ground and the German front line at Breslau Point was on another, with a small valley in between them.

On the left side of the attack area, to help nullify the Germans defending the craters, it had been proposed that a bombardment of heavy howitzers would take place twenty-four hours before the attack. Because of the closeness of the two front lines at this point, however, it was not possible, even with the most accurate fire, to carry this out without withdrawing the British troops already in position, which would not have been a practical proposition. This would also certainly have alerted the Germans to the timing of the coming attack. It was proposed, instead to use Livens Flame Projectors and, although as we have seen, these were successful in stifling resistance on the western edge of the crater field, they left the eastern edge largely undamaged.

The task of taking this point was given to a company of the 7/Buffs, who, although technically in support, was specifically chosen for this task. When the British barrage lifted at 7.30 am, instead of being able to clear out the craters, it was immediately pinned down by fierce machine-gun fire, from the crater field and from Breslau Trench. This also meant that when the 7/Queens attempted to cross No Man's Land it, too, was met with a withering fire as was the 7/Royal West Kents who followed up an hour later. By this time, the brigades to the right and the left of the 55th were making excellent progress and the whole of the attack was in danger of faltering unless an advance could be made.

With great fortitude, however, the 7/Buffs eventually managed to overcome the Germans in the Carnoy Craters, after some desperate hand to hand fighting, which eventually allowed the advance to continue, despite fierce German fire from Breslau Support Trench and the eastern end of The Loop. Particularly successful in this fighting was Sergeant Upton:

> *There was one man, Sergeant P.G. Upton, whom eye-witnesses credit with killing ten Germans in this crater fighting. During the two hours of intense conflict he led an attack upon a concrete machine-gun emplacement and killed all the detachment. Sergeant Upton was a small man, full of confidence in himself. He took his soldiering very seriously.*[19]

By this time, the Carnoy Craters were cleared and the Brigade commander, Sir T.D. Jackson, realising the necessity to push forward as soon as possible, ordered the reserve battalion, the 7/Royal West Kents, to reinforce the attack, but its commanding officer had already anticipated this need and the battalion was able to support the 7/Queens as it gradually advanced.

Despite constant fire from The Loop, the three battalions from 55 Brigade were then able to push forward, which relieved the pressure on the fourth battalion of the Brigade, the 8/East Surreys, which was in serious trouble near Train Alley. The 7/Queens, meanwhile, was still held up by machine-gun fire coming from the left. However, by this time, Pommiers Redoubt had fallen and Montauban itself was being seriously threatened and the German defenders in Breslau Support Trench, (principally from Infanterie-Regiment Nr. 62 and Reserve Infanterie-Regiment Nr. 109) realising that they were in danger of being outflanked, began to pull back. Consequently, shortly after 10.00 am, the 7/Royal West Kents was able to enter the western end of Train Alley, so relieving the 8/East Surreys and capturing 90 prisoners.

This only left the German stronghold at the junction of Back Trench and Breslau Alley to deal with and, after bringing up the divisional pioneer battalion, the 8/Royal Sussex Regiment, to add weight to the assault, the position was attacked on three sides by parties of bombers and it eventually fell in the early afternoon, two officers and 150 men being captured. These were mainly from 6. Bayerisches Reserve Infanterie-Regiment and one wounded soldier was actually captured chained to his machine-gun. This gave the allied propaganda machine the opportunity to offer the world the theory that German troops had to be forced to fight by such procedures, or that troops from penal battalions were used in the front line. It is more likely, however, that this was an act of personal bravado, rather than one of official military strategy.[20] One sergeant of the 7/Queens later wrote home of his experiences in the captured trenches:

We had carried the first two lines and on getting into the third, we saw the Germans coming up from the two exits of a deep dug-out and going down the trench. Our platoon commander got into the trench and picked the Huns off as they came out. He had a mouth of the dug out on either side of him, say 15 yards away. A German would rush out of No. 1 exit – over he went. Then one would come out of No. 2 exit, and over he went. Our officer was as cool as a cucumber – he simply turned from right to left and fired just as if he was in a shooting saloon. It was the best bit of fancy shooting I've seen – all prizes, no blanks.

After we'd finished off that bit of business – it only took about a minute – off we went again, and I got shot in the shoulder, but I saw our officer and the rest of the boys going forward as if they were off to a picnic. [21]

The attacking force of the 7/Queens, fortified by the arrival of the 7/Buffs, victors of the Carnoy Crater slaughter, then pressed forward to the approaches of the Mametz to Montauban road, which they reached at about 3 pm. There they made contact with the other battalions from 55 Brigade which had reached the road at about noon. They immediately came under heavy machine-gun fire from in front of Montauban Alley, however, which was their final objective. At this time there was a gap between them and the men of 53 Brigade on their left. However, by bringing up Stokes Mortars, they pounded the enemy line and the strangely-named Second Lieutenant Tortiss of the 7/Queens led a storming party which exploited the gap made by the mortars to take that portion of the enemy trench which lay in front of them, and then went on to capture a machine-gun position at the western edge of Montauban itself.

Second Lieutenant H.J. Tortiss, who on reaching Blind Alley, which he knew to be occupied by the enemy, took forward a bombing party. So many bombs had been thrown during the morning that only one bomb per man could be given out. But the party captured the trench and twelve Germans with it. In Montauban itself was a post held by three machine-guns. For three hours it held out. Lieutenant Tortiss, who had the Maxse dictum – 'Kill Germans' – ingrained in him, made a dash at them. He and his dozen men got right among the enemy, bayoneted several of them and ended in possession of the post. [22]

By 5.15 pm, the whole of Montauban Alley was in British hands. Although the 8/East Surreys had finally reached the Mametz to Montauban road at about mid-day, it had not had an easy time. The first

A bombing party off to the attack.

problem came with the terrain over which it was supposed to advance. As we have seen, the start line of the Battalion was on one piece of high ground and the German front line at Breslau Point was on another, with a small valley in between. Thus it had to cross the valley and attack up towards Breslau Trench and Breslau Point, where the German front line also took a change of direction to maintain the domination of the high ground at that point. This meant that, until the Kingston-on-Thames men had reached the high ground on which the Germans were expertly positioned, they were at the total mercy of the defenders. Furthermore, the German front line to the east of Breslau Point, named Valley Trench, was at a distance of some 400 yards from the attacking soldiers, as it followed the contours of the valley there, which meant that they could be fired on from ahead and enfiladed from the right.

One of the more famous stories of the Great War is that of Captain W.P. Nevill, commanding officer of B Company of the Battalion, who, renowned for his sense of humour and his joie de vivre, had purchased footballs on a previous home leave. His intention was that in order to take the men's minds off the impossibility of the attack and to instil a certain confidence into them, the footballs should be kicked by his attacking platoons across No Man's Land and into the German trenches. [23]

Just before the British barrage lifted, the East Surreys had moved into No Man's Land, and at 7.30 am Captain Nevill himself 'kicked off'. This action was later described by Private L. S. Price of the divisional pioneer battalion, the 8/Royal Sussex Regiment :-

As the gun-fire died away I saw an infantryman climb onto the parapet into No Man's Land, beckoning others to follow. As he did so he kicked off a football; a good kick, the ball rose and travelled well towards the German line. That seemed to be the signal to advance. [8]

Immediately the East Surreys left the British front line, however, inevitable machine-gun fire opened up on them from in front, from the right and from a fortified position known as The Warren, up the upward slope towards Montauban itself. Being exposed as the Battalion was, the casualties were immediately high and included Captain Nevill and his company second-in-command, Lieutenant R.E. Soames. The footballs did reach the German trenches, however.

Although the Battalion took Breslau Trench, it was then pinned down, largely by fire from The Warren and from The Loop on its left and as the 7/Queens, next to it in the line, had similarly been held up, it was not able to move. Realising that it was vital that it was able to support the attack of the 90 Brigade on its right, which was scheduled to take Montauban itself, its commanding officer Major, (acting Lieutenant Colonel) A.P.B. Irwin managed to rally those men not already killed or wounded and led them forward towards the Battalion objective at Train Alley. He was helped in this by the fact that by this time the advance of the 30th Division on the right had threatened to outflank the Germans in The Warren and they had started to pull back. As a result, he and Second Lieutenant C. Janion and their men, together with some of the support troops from the 7/Buffs, were able to push bombing parties forward and take the trenches just short of Train Alley, where they were eventually joined by the 7/Royal West Kents.

Apart from Colonel Irwin, Second Lieutenant Janion was the only unwounded officer in all of the three leading companies. Irwin, the Battalion Medical Officer, Captain E.C. Gimson, RAMC (always thought of as a sort of 'unofficial' second in command of the Battalion) and Second Lieutenant Janion were all awarded the Distinguished Service Order for their splendid work that day. With such few effective men left, it was difficult to organise any further assaults of any value, but as Montauban fell, the Battalion was eventually able to push forward and, with the Royal West Kents, reach the Mametz to

The newly captured Montauban Alley, after the British had restored it.

Montauban road at about midday. The 8/East Surreys War Diary relates the jubilation of the victory, after so many losses:-

At 12.35 p.m. Major Irwin arrived with Headquarters and took command of all troops of the 55th Brigade West of MONTAUBAN. A Number of Buffs and West Kents had arrived by this time and were ordered to hold on in MONTAUBAN ALLEY with the E. Surreys in close support. When Lieut HEATON, 7th Queens arrived he was ordered to extend the line to the left so that the whole Brigade objective was reached by 1.30 p.m.. Captain Gimson had arrived close behind Major Irwin, and later L/C. Brame turned up with a bottle of champagne to be drunk in MONTAUBAN 'ON DER TAG' This bottle was sent round from Officer to Officer, those who shared it being Major Irwin, Captain Gimson, Captain Brown, 2/Lieut Derrick, 2/Lieut Janion, 2/Lieut Thorley, 2/Lieut Wightman, 2/Lieut Alcock and Captain Clare. In fact all the East Surrey Officers engaged in the attack who had not been killed or wounded. [24]

With 55 Brigade's successes in taking Montauban Alley, the 18th Division's objectives had all been met.

The 21 Brigade Attack

21 Brigade, under the command of Brigadier-General Hon. C. J. Sackville-West, was on the western edge of the 30th Division assault, with the 18/King's on the left, the 19/Manchesters on the right, the 2/Green Howards in support and the 2/Wiltshires in reserve.

As we have already seen, 21 Brigade was originally a Regular Army brigade, 'swapped' from the 7th Division, to 'stiffen' the New Army 30th Division. It seems strange, therefore, that for what was to be perhaps the most important attack of the war to date, the two first assaulting infantry battalions would be the relatively inexperienced City Battalions from Liverpool and Manchester. Sackville-West was certainly no fool, however, but a very experienced officer, [25] so the choice must have been quite deliberate. Perhaps he considered

82

that if the City Battalions became held up, then there was always the Regular Army experience behind them to help out. It is equally possible, however, that the idea came from Lieutenant-General Congreve, the Corps Commander or Major General Shea, the Divisional Commander. Whoever made this decision, however, it can not have impressed the career soldiers of the Regular Army battalions, whose future chance of promotion, as with all career soldiers, lay with proving themselves worthy in successful battles. Nevertheless, as events were to prove, the experience of the 2/Green Howards and 2/Wiltshires was not called upon or needed.

The task of all the brigades of the 30th Division was to wrest the village of Montauban itself from the Germans and that of 21 Brigade was to take and hold the eastern portion of Train Alley and then move onward to take and hold Glatz Redoubt. This was potentially the most difficult of all the 30th Division's attacks as No Man's Land was at its widest in the Sackville-West's area, which meant that at that point, the attacking troops had to cross over 500 yards to get to the German front line.

The 18/King's was waiting in assembly trenches just to the east of Talus Boisé at 7.22 am, when the Brigade Trench Mortar Batteries began to register devastating hits on the German front line from the ends of the Russian Saps, whose tops had just been exposed to the open. Many of the waiting infantrymen would use these saps as a quick route into No Man's Land. The artillery of the 30th Division and the trench mortars had done such a good job that when the whistles blew at 7.30 am, many of the 18th were already well into No Man's Land and soon occupied what was left of the German front line, known as Silesia Trench at this point, before the Bavarian defenders had even got to the surface from their deep dug-outs. The soldiers of the 6. Bayerisches Reserve Infanterie-Regiment, had already suffered a grievous blow when a heavy howitzer shell, probably French, had penetrated the roof of a command post in Glatz Redoubt and killed nearly all the regimental staff who were there.

Leaving 'mopper-uppers' to pick up the confused and dazed Germans who began to emerge into the light, the first and second waves of the Kingsmen moved through Silesia Trench towards the German support line and immediately came under machine-gun fire from the high ground on the right. This gun was eventually silenced, however, and the support line cleared by bombers. By this time, the Germans on the higher ground behind the front and reserve lines, and as yet untouched by the main British bombardment, had begun to recover. Machine-gunners mounted their guns on the trench parapets and, concealed by hedges, began to open up onto the third and fourth waves of attacking Liverpool Pals as they left their assembly trenches and tried to cross No Man's Land. One such gun, firing from The Warren, on the left, just inside the 18th Division's territory, probably caused nearly all of the Battalion's 500 casualties that day. Another was protected by snipers and bombers at the junction of Alt Trench and Alt Alley and threatened to hold up the advance.

Having crossed No Man's Land, Captain A. de B. Adam led his men forward to try to silence it, was shot down by a sniper almost immediately but despite his wound still struggled forward before being hit again. Second Lieutenant G.A. Herdman, already slightly wounded by a German shell in the early morning of 1 July, then took up the challenge but he was hit by a German stick grenade which blew his head off. His father later related the incident as told to him by Herdman's platoon sergeant, J. Gaskell. [26]

The platoon was 44 strong when they went over the parapet at 7.30. They were the third wave, but by the time they reached the third German trench he says George was leading what was left of the battalion. ..... They paused together at the left hand end of 'Alt' trench where it comes to the little valley containing the light railway and were there together Capt. Adam, Lieut. Fitzbrown, George, Gaskell and the Sergeant-Major. These five laughed together and congratulated each other on having got through so far. The three officers were all killed soon afterwards.

Captured German trench after the bombardment.

Further to our left, on the other side of the valley, our next Division was held up and did not make so much progress, and as a result the enemy were able to fire on our left flank, and did much damage to the battalion, and bombs came from a hidden trench running down the side of the valley through some bushes. George at once got a small party of bombers – odd men who were near, not all of his own platoon - and led them down this branch or communication trench leading to elaborate German dug-outs, and there he 'ran full tilt' into the enemy, and was killed at once by a German bomb, which struck his head and must have caused instantaneous death. He was otherwise uninjured.

Before himself being killed by another German grenade, Captain Adam still found the strength to call up a party of bombers to try to capture the position and they, under the command of Lieutenant H.C. Watkins, managed to bomb their way through Alt Trench and Alt Alley, and dash along Train Alley, killing or capturing all the German defenders who got in their way. In all, one officer and thirty men were taken prisoner, chiefly from Reserve Infanterie-Regiment Nr. 109, which should have been relieved in the line the previous night, but could not be got away because of the British bombardment. This action virtually outflanked the Germans in The Warren, although they still held out until about 9.30 am, but it allowed a clear way through to the western edge of Glatz Redoubt.

Professor Herdman described the end of his son's story :-

Gaskell (who was then sending up flares to show our artillery we had taken the trench), had followed at once with other men, and says he found George's body within three minutes of the time he had left him at 'Alt' Trench. He regarded it as a 'very brave thing to do' to lead the men down that hidden trench.

After they had cleared the enemy out, he came back, and wrapped George's body in a blanket and laid it in a dug-out, and then two days after, under Lieutenant Watkins' orders, he brought the body to where they had the other dead officers who were buried together. Gaskell did not see where they were buried.[27]

With the machine-gun silenced and the British barrage moving further up the slope towards Montauban itself, the remnants of the 18th Battalion were able to push forwards on their right flank and together with the 19/Manchesters, take their objective, Glatz Redoubt, which fell to them at about 8.35 am. Because of their depleted numbers, however, they were unable to do much else, other than prepare a defence against any possible German counter-attack

The 19/Manchesters, on the right of the 18/King's, fared better. Like the Kingsmen, they too followed the eastern slope of Railway Valley and encountered little resistance as they crossed No Man's Land and in some places, took the Germans totally by surprise:

> *It was clear that they had been taken by surprise, for many of them were barefooted, none of them had any equipment. When there was no attack at 4 a.m., they were then told that they could lie down and have a rest, as the British would not now come out till four in the afternoon. It is abundantly clear that the famous German intelligence department was absolutely at fault in the southern sector of the great battle.*[28]

It is also likely that, as many of the Bavarian defenders had only just taken over the front line trenches, they were not yet ready for a strong defence of the position. One of these defenders, Reservist Michael Theurlein of 6. Bayerisches Reserve Infanterie-Regiment, later described what happened to him that morning and afterwards:

> *I was very badly wounded during a struggle with hand grenades at the beginning of the attack when British troops advanced into our trenches. My right leg was smashed and my arms and head were bleeding from many wounds. I had the misfortune to stay like that for one and a half days without being dressed until I was found by an English Army Medical Officer. I was taken to a field ambulance by some men and still today I give the greatest praise and gratitude to the English people who attended me so well.*
>
> *I was taken to England on 9th July to a hospital near Dartford and I stayed there for twelve months until I was able to walk with two sticks. The treatment in this hospital was also very good, especially a nurse Williams who took care of me for six to eight months without any trouble to her. She dressed my wounds and those of my comrades every day without fatigue.*
>
> *When I recovered, I was sent to Dorchester Camp for five months and then to another camp at Brockton for some weeks. From this place, I was exchanged as an unfit soldier to wonderful Switzerland.*[29]

Private A. Andrews related the sight which greeted the first wave of the 19/Manchesters:

> *I jumped into a German trench, what was left of it near a dugout door. In the doorway there was a big barrel. As soon as I jumped in a German jumped out from behind this barrel. I was*

already on guard and had my bayonet on his chest, he was trembling and looked half mad with his hands above his head saying something to me which I did not understand at all. I could make out that he did not want me to kill him. It was here that I noticed my bayonet was broken, I could not have stuck him. Of course I had one 'up the chimney' as we call it, you only have to press the trigger the bullet being in the breach. I pointed to his belt and bayonet, he took these off, his hat, water bottle, emptied his pockets offering them to me. Just then one of my mates was coming up the trench, "Get out of the way, Andy, leave him to me. I'll give him one to himself", meaning that he would throw a bomb at him which would have blew [sic] him to pieces. I said "Come here." He was on his knees in front of me, fairly pleading. I said, "He's an old man." He looked 60 at the finish. I pointed my thumb towards our lines never taking the bayonet off his chest. He jumped up and with his hands above his head run [sic] out of the trench towards our lines calling out all the time. He was trembling from head to foot, frightened to death. This was the only German I ever let off and I have never regretted it, because I believed he could have done me quite easily as I jumped into the trench.[30]

Although the 19/Manchesters was also troubled by the machine-gun firing from The Warren, it was able to wait for the British barrage on Alt Trench to lift and then, at about 7.45 am, it occupied its allotted part of the trench without heavy loss. From there, it, together with the 18/Kings, which had by this time overcome the problems on its left, was able to occupy the objective for the day, Glatz Redoubt, on schedule, at about 8.35 am.

Upon reaching Glatz Redoubt, smoke candles and red flares were ignited to show that the objective had been reached and these acted as a dual pointer and cover for the advancing men of 90 Brigade. The Battalion then began to consolidate the captured position, by changing the direction of the trench parapet, building a new fire step to face the enemy, clearing communication trenches to the rear to bring up much needed supplies of water and war materiel and digging new protective trenches which would not be marked on the old German maps.

Meanwhile, the support battalion of the Brigade, the 2/Green Howards, had literally run into trouble. Its task was to hold and consolidate the German front and support lines once captured, to allow the 18/King's and 19/Manchesters to move forward and take Glatz Redoubt. The Yorkshiremen followed the Lancashire battalions across

No Man's Land and soon came under the fire of the enfilading German machine-guns firing from the left, which had caused the Kingsmen so much trouble. Only about 30 men from the attacking two companies reached Breslau Trench and most of the Battalion's 200 casualties that day were sustained at this point. Nevertheless, the survivors began the task of consolidation, but:

> *Whilst thus engaged a German machine-gun, which had escaped notice up to now, suddenly opened fire; this was located by Lance-Corporal W. Parkin, who made for it single handed, killed the two men composing the detachment and captured the gun; this was then at once handed to the Brigade Machine Gun Company, who brought it into action against the enemy.*[31]

For the rest of the day the 2/Green Howards held onto and consolidated the newly captured trenches but in certain places encountered great difficulty, as the British bombardment had all but obliterated the German lines.

The task of the reserve battalion, The 2/Wiltshires, was twofold. It was to keep the assaulting battalions of 21 Brigade continuously supplied with ammunition and war materiel to consolidate captured trenches and it was also to man the jumping off trenches with a skeleton force, once they had been vacated by the attackers. It also held the British front line until the last possible time before the attack, to give the assaulting battalions as much rest as possible. Therefore, it had been relieved there by the 18/King's on the night of 27 June for the original attack the next day, but when this was postponed it took over the line again until the eve of 1 July.

Major W.S. Shepherd, M.C. later described the work of the Battalion on that fateful day: [32]

> *Although not actually in the assault, the Wiltshires, especially 'A' 'B' and 'C' Companies had a hard day. As soon as Glatz redoubt had been taken these companies set out with all sorts of food, ammunition, picks, shovels, etc., and, after depositing these with one or the other of the front battalions, they returned to fetch another load and repeat the operation. Backwards and forwards they went, over the shell-torn ground and under the trying July sun, bearing their heavy burdens.*

> *The distance from the source of supply to the captured position was about one and a half miles. There was no path, and the whole way the ground was pitted with deep shell holes. Many gaping trenches lay between the carrying parties and their destination, and these had to be crossed, each man with his load.*

The Germans put in a good deal of wild shelling, of which these parties had to run the gauntlet. But they stuck at it all day long, each company doing many journeys and thus enabling the ground won to be safely consolidated.

The 89 Brigade Attack

89 Brigade, under the command of Brigadier-General Hon. F.C. Stanley, the Earl of Derby's brother, was on the eastern edge of the 30th Division assault with the 20/King's on the left, the 17/King's on the right, the 2/Bedfords in support and the 19/King's in reserve. The Brigade was on the extreme right of the British Army on the Western Front and on its right was the French 153e Régiment d'Infanterie, 39th Division, XX Corps. The XX Corps was known as *'Le Corps de Fer'* or The Iron Corps, because of its steadiness at Verdun.

Just before 7.30 am the 20/King's was waiting apprehensively for the Brigade trench mortar batteries to stop firing in assembly trenches just north of Maricourt village. No Man's Land in front of it was between 400 and 500 yards wide and none of the men wanted to be caught crossing it when the main British bombardment on the German front line – at the junction of Silesia Trench and Favière Trench, – lifted. Despite general orders to advance at a walking pace, when the whistles blew, the men dashed across the gap in quick time in extended company lines with about 100 yards in between each one. Finding most of the German wire cut by allied howitzer fire, they dashed across the front line and through the Silesia Support Line and, hardly pausing, crossed the German reserve line at Alt Trench and by 8 am took possession of their first objective, Casement Trench.

At this point, the Battalion had to halt and wait, as its main objective, Dublin Trench,

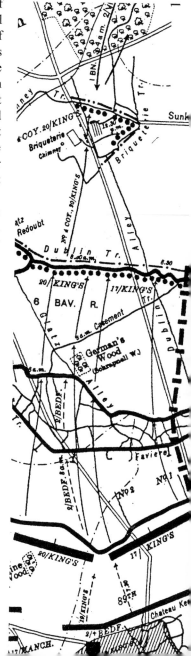

View of Montauban brickyard taken on 26 October 1915.

was still being pounded by British and French artillery. When this barrage moved on, however, the Kingsmen were able to move forward again and by 8.30 am take and hold the portion of Dublin Trench ahead of them, without much serious opposition, as most of the German defenders had retreated to the rear and those that remained were happy to surrender. Lance Corporal J. Quinn of the 20th Battalion described them:

> *There were great numbers gave themselves up as prisoners, and they did it in anything but a manly way. ..... Most of us out here have a great respect for their artillery, but so far a contempt for their infantry.*[33]

The western end of Dublin Trench connected with Glatz Redoubt and as this, too, had fallen by the time the 20th men were beginning to consolidate their gain, it was possible to move along the trench and make contact with the 18/King's and 19/Manchesters who were also consolidating their capture. One of the most important tasks was to dig a new trench forward of Dublin Trench, as the German gunners on the Guillemont Ridge knew the exact range of their former reserve lines. Lance Corporal Quinn described the situation:

> *When our line pushed on further, we found that the German fourth line was too congested so we had to dig ourselves in. The shelling was very bad just here, but not many of our fellow got hit. It was later on, when we were holding the trench we had dug, that we had a hot time, for the German artillery picked up the range very quickly, and were soon dropping shells right over the parapet.*[33]

The 20th Battalion held onto Casement trench whilst the battle for Montauban was going on to the north, but once this had fallen orders were received from Brigade Headquarters, at about 11.50 am, to proceed with the second phase of its attack – the capture of the Briqueterie, which stood either side of the road which connected

Bernafay Wood to Maricourt. A briefing for the attack was given at the corner of Germans Wood, which had fallen to the 17th Battalion some three hours earlier and then at 12.20 pm, Captain C. Orford led No. 4 Company into the assault, following a fierce 30 minute artillery bombardment of the position, which began at noon.

The brickworks at Montauban which the Germans were using as an O.P. was destroyed by artillery fire, and was the objective of the 20th Bn. King's Liverpool Regt.

SECRET.

Copy No. 1.

20th Bn. The King's Regt.

Operation Order No. 45.

Reference Trench Map 1/10,000

1.7.16.

Intention. 1. At 12.34 pm. today No.4 Co. will capture the BRIQUETERIN & will at once consolidate as directed in Op. Order 40. No.3 Co. will send forward the Bombing Party detailed in Op. Order No.40 to bomb down NORD ALLEY to Pt.87 (its junction with CHIMNEY TRENCH. These will bomb down CHIMNEY TRENCH as No.4 Co. advances & must indicate their position by their flag.

Artillery. 2. Artillery lifts off BRIQUETERIN at 12.30 p.m.

3. The Strong Point 2.

Acknowledge.

H. W. COBHAM, LT. COL.

Comg. 20th Bn. King's Regt.

Issued to all concerned 11.55 a.m.

Helped by a party of bombers from No. 3 Company, who attacked the position from the left flank down Nord Alley and Chimney Trench, the Briqueterie fell, after a brief fight, at 12.34 pm, when the barrage had lifted. [34]

The colonel and four other officers, (including the adjutant) from the headquarters staff of 3. Oberschlesisches Infanterie-Regiment Nr. 62, the commander and observer of Feldartillerie-Regiment von Clausewitz (1. Oberschlesisches) Nr. 21, and forty soldiers were captured there, as well as two machine-guns, many important intelligence documents and maps. The capture of the Briqueterie was one of the most important gains of the day, as it not only reduced a German stronghold on the right flank of the British front but also eventually allowed for the reduction and capture of Bernafay Wood.[35]

When zero came, the 17th Battalion had much the same start as the 20th. Its objective was also Dublin Trench, but the eastern end, which led into Dublin Redoubt. Dublin Redoubt was the objective of the French 3e Bataillon, 153e R.I., on the Kings' right. As the Kingsmen crossed No Man's Land they encountered very little shelling and virtually no machine-gun fire and found the wire on the German front line, Favière Trench, was totally cut. This was probably because of the work of the French heavy howitzers on their right, as the French artillery had learned valuable lessons on reducing earthworks through bitter experience during the fighting at Verdun.

The commander of the 17th Battalion, Lieutenant-Colonel B.C. Fairfax, left the assembly trenches with the second wave of advancing troops and at much the same time, so did the commander of the 3e Bataillon, 153e R.I., Commandant Le Petit. In the symbolic spirit of entente, they led their respective troops across No Man's Land arm in arm. Crossing Favière Trench and the eastern end of Train Alley, the 17th Battalion surged forward and, by 8 am, had taken Germans Wood (known to the Germans as Schrapnel Wald), on its line of advance. There it captured 30 Germans from 3. Oberschlesisches Infanterie-Regiment Nr. 62, who were quickly sent to the rear as the Battalion pushed on to take Casement Trench. Pausing, then, like its comrades of the 20th Battalion, for the British barrage on Dublin Trench to lift, it took and occupied its objective, Dublin Trench, at about 8.30 am. At about the same time, the French 153e had taken Dublin Redoubt and the two battalion commanders met at the eastern edge of Dublin Trench and embraced in the spirit of unity, comradeship and victory.

Lieutenant E.W. Willmer of the 17th, but not actually involved in the attack witnessed the advance:

On the first day, I was in the support line and got a marvellous view of all that happened. It was a lovely sunny morning and promptly at 7.30, our barrage lifted from the German front line to their support line, and waves of British troops left the trenches and walked out into No Man's Land, in extended line, with bayonets fixed and rifles at the carry. There was no hurry, and so far as our battalion was concerned, very little resistance. Our casualties were small and we gained our objectives without trouble, and dug in at our new position. Further north of course, things were very different, and the casualties were appalling. [33]

All that remained for the 17th for the rest of the day, was to consolidate the position it had taken against possible counter-attack and the inevitable shelling that would come when the Germans had recovered from the shock of losing Montauban. Consequently, a fresh line was dug about 100 yards to the north of Dublin Trench, with war materiel brought up by the 19/King's, whose men were acting as carriers. This new trench saved many lives when the German barrage eventually fell on Dublin Trench. In the afternoon, Battalion Headquarters was moved to the old Favière Support Trench and shared with 3e Bataillon of the 153e R.I. so close was the inter-allied co-operation by this time.

It is probable that the 17/King's was the most successful battalion anywhere on the Somme front that day, if success is measured in ground taken and lives lost, for it took all it objectives without the death, on 1 July anyway, of a single member of the Battalion. Even those who died of wounds later were in very small numbers compared with the carnage elsewhere. [36]

Meanwhile the 2/Bedfords, in close support, had not been idle. As one would expect from a Regular Army unit, the Battalion followed up behind the battalions from Liverpool with total professionalism. The account of the day's action was first told in the Regimental Magazine, *The Wasp*:

At 7.30 a.m., while it was still so hazy that we could not see the German trenches from our assembly positions, the advance began. It was a wonderful sight to see the men extend and, in spite of the enemy shell fire, march on just as if they were at an Aldershot field day. By 8 a.m. the German front lines, Faviere and Silesia trenches, were taken and the leading battalions were pushing on to Casement Trench, Alt Alley and Glatz Alley.

B Company (Captain H.A.W. Pearse) and C. Company (Captain R.O. Wynne) followed 100 yards behind the leading

German prisoners on their way to the cages.

battalions and established themselves in Faviere and Silesia
Support Trenches, while the artillery bombarded Dublin Trench.
When this was captured these two companies moved up to
Casement Trench, while A Company (Captain C.G. Tyler) and D
Company (Captain L.F. Beal) took over the garrison of Faviere
and Silesia Support trenches. ..... .

Second Lieutenants B. Gaze and A. Young and 60 men of D
Company followed the third wave of the leading battalions to
clean up the German trenches and dug-outs. They split up into

*small parties of a non-commissioned officer and 5 men, each
told off to work up definite sections of the enemy trenches. Their
work was done most satisfactorily, some 300 prisoners and 4
machine guns being captured, after which they rejoined their
company.*[37]

These prisoners were chiefly from 3. Oberschlesisches Infanterie-
Regiment Nr. 62. The rest of the day was spent in consolidation and in
the evening of 1 July the Battalion moved its headquarters up to the
former German front line, where it remained until relieved.

The 19/Kings, the Brigade reserve battalion, was stationed in the
remains of the old Maricourt Chateau and took no part in the direct
assault of the enemy lines. As soon as the enemy positions began to
fall, however, its men were used as carriers for all the war materials
needed to support the forward battalions an to enable them to
consolidate their captured positions. Lance Corporal Quinn of the 20th
Battalion paid tribute to the efforts of the carriers of the 19/Battalion
after the German support lines had fallen:

*By this time, the (19th Battalion) who were reserve carriers
for us, had now come over too, and we watched them from behind
the battered German trench as they came on with coils of barbed
wire, ammunition etc., over their shoulders.*

Sometimes you would see one of them coming forward

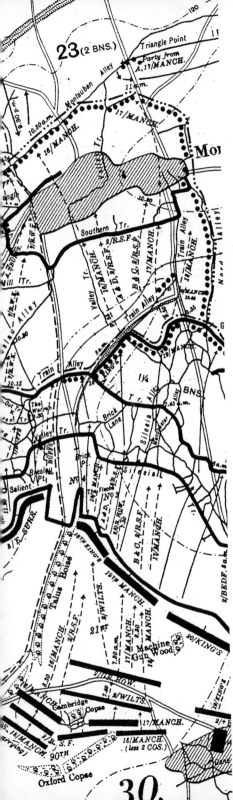

laboriously with a big load. Suddenly a 'Jack Johnson'[38] would scream over our heads and appear to burst within twenty yards of the carrier. At any rate, the smoke from it would clear away and you would again see him like the man 'off to Philadelphia', striding forward with his 'bundle on his shoulder', as though nothing had happened.[39]

By nightfall, one officer from the 19th Battalion had been wounded and thirteen other ranks had been killed, but it had kept the vital supplies moving up the line which enabled the rest of the Brigade to hold on to what it had so valiantly taken.

The 90 Brigade Attack

90 Brigade, under the command of Brigadier-General C.J. Steavenson, was given the task of taking the village of Montauban itself with the 16/Manchesters on the left, the 17/Manchesters on the right, the 2/Royal Scots Fusiliers in support and the 18/Manchesters in reserve. The whole Brigade assembled in Cambridge Copse, west of Maricourt, during the early morning of 1 July and then moved forward in time for the attack. Despite popular belief that attacks on the Somme were ordered by chaotic 'bunglers', without a real knowledge of the objectives ahead, in reality the opposite was the truth.

The whole trench system had been reproduced in facsimile at Briquemesnil.

96

Silesia Trench, Glatz Redoubt and the topography of Montauban itself, with all the streets marked out, with dummy hedges and Montauban Alley, the final objective, were there. Here, day after day, the attack was practised, there being no respite until every man was familiar with the part he had to take. On one occasion the Division carried out the operation entirely without officers, and it was effected without a hitch.[39]

It was vital if the Brigade attack were to succeed, that the German reserve line and Glatz Redoubt had fallen and once Steavenson saw the red flares set off from the former German stronghold at 8.30 am, he signalled his battalions to advance. As well as the Manchester men lighting signal flares, the task of hiding the advance up the slope from Glatz Redoubt to the village itself was given to the 4th Mortar Company of No. 5 Battalion, Special Brigade, Royal Engineers. This unit was armed with twelve four inch Stokes Mortars and, firing from the newly captured Glatz Redoubt, it laid down a smoke barrage so dense that the Germans could not see the Mancunians as they moved forward into the attack. In fact, *The Official History* reports:

German diaries ('Feld-Art. Regt No. 21') state that the smoke cloud at this time was so thick in Montauban and Caterpillar Valley that one could only see two or three yards ahead.

The objective of the 16/Manchesters - the First Manchester City Pals – was Montauban Alley and at approximately 8.30 am, the battalion left its assembly trenches – fortified by the knowledge that Glatz Redoubt was in British hands and that the French had already taken Hardecourt and Favière Wood. Before its men reached the Redoubt, however, they came across fierce machine-gun fire from The Warren on the Battalion's left. This was probably the same gun which had already

British troops taking shelter in a shallow trench.

caused so much trouble to the men of 55 and 21 Brigades.

Private C. Heaton of the 16th Battalion later related what happened:

When we got the word to advance, we just shook ourselves together and started going up the ladders, because the Liverpools had cleared their trench. I'd got five men with supplies with me and a bayonet man in front of me, who happened to be a German – Louis Alban, No. 2 Platoon, he lived at Ardwick and his family had moved years before. So Louis's getting to the top and he's supposed to go round these trenches where these German dug-outs were – my job and others was to bomb them out, but I couldn't go round a trench parapet without knowing it was clear because I couldn't carry a rifle with all I'd got – so as soon as he got on top and flexed his knees, he went down, (shot) clean through the head. ..... Alban's job was to go round a trench first and if there was a man there, a Jerry, he was to shoot him and warn me and then we'd throw our Mills bombs into the trench, but he just stood up on the top of the trench when they came round with their fire.

On the Friday night, the night before July 1, in the billets, just before we marched to the trench, we were told that if you got hit, the best thing to do was make for a shell hole and lie there until things were quiet. Well all my five were down, howling like cats and horses, screaming – they'd been hit with this fire. Now you're not supposed to give help to the wounded and the sergeant of the platoon he was shot, straight away as soon as he got on top – he was shot through the liver.

So there was a drop from the trench we started from, until you came to a Jerry communication trench. Well, I'd no men, they were all out – hundreds of them, so on the parados of the communication trench sat two officers, one was Captain Worthington and the other was Captain Elstob ..... He shouted to me 'Get some men and work along this communication trench' and I thought to myself 'How the so-and-so can I get men, they're all dead. There's only dead men who can do anything for me.' – there was nobody following on either.

So anyway, I started up this trench and the first one I came to had about seven in who were very glad to give themselves up – 'Kamerad' – I said 'Hands up' and sent them on their way and I cleared that trench the best I could, because it was all nearly flat, with our shelling. I was just getting into the open again when I get one in the arm and then one of our fellows came up and he cut my sleeve off and did my damage up and I got down to Maricourt. [40]

By this time the rest of the 16/Manchesters was approaching Train Alley fifteen minutes before schedule and had to wait for the British barrage on Montauban to lift. During this wait, the position of the German machine-gun was discovered and a Lewis gun team from the 16th put it out of action – the German gun crew firing up until the very last moment before it was wiped out.

As the barrage lifted, the Manchester men flooded forwards and into Glatz Redoubt before moving on, still under the cover of the smoke barrage laid down by the Royal Engineers. Their arrival there had disastrous results for at least one Liverpool Pal of the 18th Battalion who had been 'souveniring' like his comrade Private W. Gregory:

> *Then we went down into the dugout to do a bit of 'souveniring'. The Germans must have left pretty quickly because they hadn't even taken their coats, so we went through the pockets. I got a German soldier's pay book, some buttons and a spiked helmet. ..... I hung on to the pay book and the officer's helmet, which my mother later threw out because it had blood stains on the inside.*
>
> *Another of our lads also got a spiked helmet which he put on his head. He was still wearing it when we went back up to the trench, and he was larking around with it. Just then, one of the Manchesters who were coming up behind us, came round the traverse, and seeing him with helmet on, must have thought he was a German, and shot him dead. It couldn't be helped, it was just one of those things that happens in war.* [33]

At this stage, there was some discussion at Corps headquarters as to whether the attack should be allowed to continue as 55 Brigade on the left was still struggling, and if it did not succeed, it would leave any advance force from the 30th Division out on a very dangerous limb. This was especially so as the French on the right had decided to go no further. However, it was eventually decided that as the 30th Division was doing so well, 55 Brigade would only benefit from a victory at Montauban. Consequently, the 90 Brigade attack was ordered to proceed and as the barrage lifted, the 16/Manchesters, by this time mixed up with the 17th and the 2/Royal Scots Fusiliers, swept up the final slope through gaps in Southern Trench and into Montauban itself, just after 10.00 am.

The 17/Manchesters had also left its assembly trenches at about

8.30 am, and suffered similarly from The Warren machine-gun and from the German shelling which did no great damage, but nevertheless wounded the Battalion Commander, Lieutenant-Colonel H.A. Johnson. Once the Battalion reached Glatz Redoubt, it too had to halt to await further orders and for the British barrage on Montauban to lift. Second Lieutenant K. Callan-Macardle later told of the conditions there:

> The ground was so rough and broken with shell holes that when I lay down under our barrage I found myself ahead of the first line – I had four men left. The 17th had advanced too quickly. We had done it all at the slowest walk and been quite unchequed [sic] – so we lay down for forty minutes, under the shells, waiting. Waiting is hard. We were to rush the village at 9.56.[30]

Soon the 17th, also, was to break through Southern Trench and enter the village itself and, mindful of the many practice attacks made at Briquemesnil:

> On finally reaching the objective, a platoon humorist, bowed under his heterogeneous assortment of burdens, was heard to remark : 'Now we'll go back and do it all over again before tea.'.[39]

The Battalion then pushed forward through the village and by the late morning, some of A Company had reached as far forward as a position at the northern end of Monatauban Alley, known as Triangle Point.

Meanwhile, the men of the 2/Royal Scots Fusiliers, had not been slow to use the benefits of their training and experience. Like their Regular Army 89 Brigade comrades in the 2/Bedfords, they were determined to make their mark on the battle. In point of fact, the whole of the 90 Brigade attack was under the command of the C.O. of the 2/Royal Scots Fusiliers, Lieutenant-Colonel R.K. Walsh.

At 8.30 am the Battalion left its trenches behind Cambridge Copse and closely followed the two Manchester battalions up the slope towards Montauban. Although in support, the Battalion played an active part in the capture of the village. By the time that the Manchester battalions were held up waiting for the barrage on the village to lift, the Scots had caught up with them and, certainly by the time the final assault on Montauban commenced, all three battalions were mixed up and undoubtedly rushed the objective together. The history of the battalion is curiously reticent about this feat or arms and merely states:

> Montauban fell early in the day to the Scots Fusiliers and the Manchesters, and Colonel Walsh was made officer commanding

the village. Owing to brigade headquarters being so far back, he practically commanded the brigade during the operations.[41]

The Battalion War Diary is hardly more forthcoming. In the passage dealing with the capture of the village, it merely states that at 10.15 am:

'A' Coy had reached the centre Keep and the remaining three Coys had occupied the trench South of the village (SOUTH TRENCH) by 10.30 a.m. and the whole Battalion started consolidating. ..... The NETTOYEUR[42] *platoons after clearing the village rejoined their own Coys, one platoon taking 28 prisoners.*

This lack of a detailed sequence of events is probably all one could expect from a regular Army unit for whom, professionally, one battle had no more import than the next, but it is almost certainly one of the reasons why the part the 2/Royal Scots Fusiliers played in the capture of the village has never been properly recognised. After all, most of the post war histories were taken, initially at least, from battalion war diaries.[43]

However, in a letter written home on the 17th July 1916, one Royal Scots Fusilier, Lance Corporal R. Kendall, who was present at the capture of Montauban wrote the following:

The General said that he could not in words let alone on paper express his admiration for the work performed by this battalion. All the regiments in our Brigade call us the 'Boys of the Village' because we took a village that the Germs [sic] *had fortified for 15 months and what they thought was impregnable but the Fus. said 'not likely'.*[43, 45]

The village was Montauban, of course and if the regiments in 90 Brigade were still referring to the Battalion as the 'Boys of the Village' by the middle of the month, then it must have been for good reason. Moreover, another account written by Private R. Sim, to author Martin Middlebrook in the early 1970s, for possible inclusion in his book The First Day on the Somme but not subsequently used, is even more illuminating:

Germans, cut off by the British bombardment, emerged from their cellar dugouts to surrender.

On the 1st July we were in position behind the Front Line near Maricourt, in support of the Manchester Regiment (the Pals battalion). At Zero Hour, I think 7.00 a.m. we went over the top, and advanced in single file, led by our platoon officer, 2 Lieutenant H. Atkins, who was later killed on the Somme on 30th July.[45] After perhaps 200 yards, we came under crossfire (rifle and machine-gun) from our left. I was hit in the region of the heart, and fell. My thoughts were, naturally, 'this is it'. Taking cover with other wounded, I stripped off my equipment, including two extra bandoliers of ammunition, and found to my amazement that although I was black and blue all over, there was no wound. On inspecting my equipment, I found that one of my bandoliers had stopped the bullet and undoubtedly had saved my life.

I immediately dressed and followed on to find my company, which I did, in the village of Montauban, which the Fusiliers had captured, the Manchesters being held up by German opposition. I am not trying to belittle the Manchesters in any way, but to give a true report. To prove this, I may tell you that our Division was relieved after a few days, and came back to 'Happy Valley'. The following day, our battalion was ordered to fall in for 'General's Parade'. While on parade, awaiting the General, we heard loud cheering some distance away from the Manchester lines. Shortly afterwards the General arrived and gave us a speech of thanks, part of which I still remember, as follows; 'Colonel Walsh, Officers and men of the Royal Scots Fusiliers, I have come to thank you for your great success. Now, although I can't congratulate you for capturing Montauban, I knew when I put you in support that anybody could capture Montauban but it would be much harder to hold it'. The general must have known by the silence of our men that something was wrong. There was no cheering, it seemed that everyone was stunned. The following day we again had 'General's Parade', and the same General arrived, but what a difference. He apologised to our regiment, and admitted he had received conflicting reports, but on making fuller enquiries, he wanted to congratulate the Royal Scots Fusiliers for capturing Montauban. I fancy I can still hear the cheering then. [8, 43]

'The General' was 90 Brigade Commander, Brigadier-General C.J. Steavenson and a transcript of his speech on that second day, 5th July 1916, survives today in the Royal Scots Fusiliers Regimental Museum in Glasgow. It states:

> *Colonel Walsh, W.Os, N.C.Os and men of the Royal Scots Fusiliers, I have come to address you again this morning because I wish to give honour where honour is due. When I spoke to you yesterday, I did not know what I know now. It is impossible, as you are aware, in an action such as you have been through, to find out just exactly what happens. From information I received yesterday, I thought it was only your Nettoyeurs who were with the assaulting lines but investigation has shown that it was the Scots Fusiliers who actually took Montauban. Colonel Walsh and Royal Scots Fusiliers, I thank you.*[43]

There is little doubt, therefore, that the Fusiliers were the driving force in the capture, which does not denigrate the part played by the men from Manchester whatsoever. The truth is, however, that no matter how brave daring and courageous were the Manchester Pals, or how intelligent were their officers, they did not have the experience under fire, the training or the steadiness of a Regular Army battalion, in what amounted to open skirmishing. Furthermore, by the time the Manchester Pals began their assault of Montauban, nearly all their officers were out of action and despite the fact that we know that an officer-less attack had been practised, the actuality must have been totally different.

The capture of Montauban – the only village taken on time throughout the whole of the Somme front on that terrible day – was an

The ruins of Montauban. It was almost impossible to trace the run of the streets.

amazing achievement and one which, with the capture of Mametz was really the only good news of the whole day. Presumably it better suited home propaganda for future recruitment to laud the efforts of the volunteer 'citizen soldiers' rather than reward the efforts of a Regular Army battalion, which would have been expected to do well, in public perception.

Whatever the reasoning behind subsequent reporting of the facts, once the intermingled troops entered Montauban it was found to be deserted – except for a fox – and the scene of devastation was total. No buildings were intact and the once famous red roof tiles had joined the rest of the village in being pulverised by the relentless hammer of the allied bombardment. The second objective for the day was Montauban Alley, however, and as some men of 90 Brigade embarked on an all round defence of the newly captured village, at about 11 am, the 16/Manchesters pushed on to capture the Alley – most of the defenders there surrendering without a fight. The scene which met the Mancunians from the captured trench was one of green open ground across Caterpillar Valley and they were amazed to see hundreds of Germans fleeing northwards up the slope towards the Bazentins. Royal Artillery forward observation officers, who had accompanied the attack, were swift to call down shell fire on these men, which was soon joined by machine-gun and rifle fire from the newly captured village.

Seeing a battery of 77 mm field guns in pits still manned by their gunners of Feldartillerie-Regiment Nr. 21, some intrepid soldiers of the 16/Manchesters rushed forward and captured them whilst shooting at their fleeing crews, who were attempting to join their comrades across the valley. Two Manchester Pals, Private H.F. Aldous and Private C.T.F. Price,[44] actually chalked their own names and their unit, on the barrels of two of the three guns. They were the first German guns to be captured anywhere on the Somme front on 1 July.

As the northern side of Montauban was fortified and consolidated by its captors and sappers of the 201st Field Company, Royal Engineers, the Germans at last began to retaliate and put down a fierce bombardment on their former positions, which lasted for most of the afternoon. This caused many casualties amongst the infantrymen and engineers.

It was obvious that any major counter-attack would come after nightfall, however, and throughout the afternoon the troops, already exhausted by the magnitude of their victory, set to

One of the 7.7cm German guns captured by Privates Aldous and Price of the 16/Manchesters beyond Montauban Alley on 1 July.

and cut fire steps, and reversed the parapets of trenches and to built strongpoints in the chalky ground, broken up and pulverised by shell fire and littered with the bricks and masonry of shattered buildings.

The reserve battalion of 90 Brigade, the 18/Manchesters, kept up a constant supply of necessary war materiel to help the new defenders accomplish this task:

> *Though other battalions won the glory that was achieved in the attack, the Eighteenth suffered a considerable mauling in performing its work. ..... The Battalion also suffered one hundred and seventy casualties of other ranks. Of these about one hundred belonged to 'C' Company, which was caught by enfilading machine-gun fire. Although the exultancy of this attack did not fall to the share of the Eighteenth, yet everyone experienced a feeling of pride in knowing that the help to which the supporting battalion had been pledged had been well and truly given. An officer describing the general work of the Brigade in this engagement said :- 'It was truly magnificent. The men advanced like veterans, and one could hardly believe they were entering upon a life and death struggle for they had the appearance of carrying out a practice manoeuvre.'* [39]

The Divisional Pioneer Battalion, the 11/South Lancashire Regiment was also brought up to dig four communication trenches across the former No Man's Land to bring up needed men and supplies if the expected counter-attack came and create positions that the Germans would not find on their artillery maps:

> *By 2.45 p.m. three of the communication trenches forward were through to the German front line at a depth of four feet, but the fourth could not be completed till much later owing to the heavy casualties caused by the enemy's shell fire. Nevertheless, all the duties allotted to the Battalion were carried out up to time, despite the number of men hit by machine-gun bullets as the various parties followed the assaulting infantry over the top into the inferno of fire that greeted them.* [46]

By 6 pm the engineers of the 201st Field Company had repaired the shattered Maricourt to Montauban road and by dusk, Montauban was quiet as both armies exhaustedly licked their wounds. Behind both front line positions, activity increased as supplies of food, water ammunition and reinforcements began their relentless movement forward.

The last act in the battle for Montauban began at 9.30 pm, with the first German counter-attack. Dispirited though the German Army was

The ruins of houses in Montauban. Note the trenches running through them.

at Montauban, its successes almost everywhere else on the British attack front must have led it to believe that Montauban could be re-taken. A mixed bunch of regiments hastily gathered together, although mostly from the already decimated 6. Bay. R.J.R., and formed up in a quarry to the north of the village roughly half way across Caterpillar Valley. Most of them had been sheltering there throughout the day and at 9.30 pm they rushed up the slope and tried to force their old position on the top of the ridge. Most of the assault was centred on the hastily fortified positions of the 16/Manchesters, who despite being on constant alert for the last twelve hours, managed to beat off the attack with rifle and machine-gun fire - no Germans actually getting near the positions. By 10.15 pm the attack had faltered and failed and the Germans disappeared back down into Caterpillar Valley. Apart from heavy German shell fire, everything then went quiet again until the early hours of the next morning:

> At 3 a.m. just as dawn was breaking, and the order to 'stand down' was about to be issued, long lines of grey figures in greatcoats and helmets were seen advancing over the ridge, shoulder to shoulder - on they came, wave after wave. The second counter attack had begun.
>
> There was no need to issue fire orders. As the Germans topped the ridge our men opened rapid fire with deadly precision, many climbing out on to the parapet to get a better field of fire. The Lewis guns served splendidly. It had been said 'You can take the village, but can you hold it?' 'We can do it,' said the men, and they did. The lonely wounded, lying among their

dead comrades on the ground behind the village under the starry sky, heard the hellish crash of the artillery preparation, and the rattle of the Lewis gun and rifle fire; saw great jets of flame among the trees of the village and the clustering rockets. 'Can they hold on – will the stampede overwhelm us?'

They (the defenders) were barely 150 strong, with 1,000 yards of communication trench to hold. There were no means of communicating to the guns direct – but the attack was broken up solely by rifle fire. Four waves had been dispersed when our artillery came into action and put up a barrage that rendered further attacks impossible. But it was not over. The enemy had broken into Montauban Alley between our extreme right post and the junction with the 17th Manchesters. 'Bombers forward' was the order. But there were no bombs. The enemy were driven back, however, and another block established on the right of the Battalion line.[39]

This was the last, almost despairing attempt by the Germans to recapture Montauban and its failure meant that the allied victory there was complete. As the day dawned fully and the British Army began to recover from the greatest disaster then experienced in its long history, the capture of Montauban shone like a beacon, lighting the path to eventual victory on the Somme. The (mainly) 'Duration Only' soldiers of Britain's citizen army had taken on the best of Germany's professional armed might and beaten them soundly.

British losses for the capture of Montauban, including all the objectives taken on XIII Corps's front, were estimated in *The Official History* (published in 1932) as just over 6,000. This was made up of 3,115 killed, wounded, missing or taken prisoner for the 18th Division and the remarkably similar figure of 3,011, for the 30th Division. German totals are not known for a variety of reason, not least of which are the fact that the German procedure for registering wounded was totally different from that of the British. However, some idea of the devastating effects of the British victory at Montauban can be gauged

Germans dash across open, but broken, ground in a counter-attack.

by the fact that Reserve Infanterie-Regiment Nr. 109 alone, is known to have lost 42 officers and 2,105 men, from a total of just over 3,000. Similarly, the captured diary of Oberstleutnant Bedell the commander of 6. Bayerisches Reserve Infanterie-Regiment, which was later used in the Bavarian Official Account, stated:

> *The troops who had so far held the lines south of Mametz and south of Montauban had sustained severe losses from intense enemy bombardment, which had been maintained for many days without a pause, and for the most part were already shot to pieces. ..... The 6th Bavarian Reserve Regiment, which on the morning of July 1st was thrown into Montauban has been completely destroyed. Of 3,500 men only 500 remained and these are for the most part men who had not taken part in the battle, plus two regimental officers and a few stragglers who turned up on the following day. All the rest are dead, wounded or missing. The regimental staff and battalion staff have all been captured in their dug-outs.*

With the continuing and eventual success of the Somme battle, Montauban was spared the total devastation that befell some of the other villages further north and only briefly saw action again as the Germans recaptured and occupied the area, from March to August 1918. Curiously, the 18th Division also played a part in its eventual liberation, as the 7/Buffs and 11/Royal Fusiliers re-captured it on 25 August 1918.

Although occupied once more by German forces from 1940 to 1944, never again in the twentieth century had it to suffer such cruel destruction and devastation in the cause of liberty.

British troops billeted in the ruins of Montauban after its capture.

Notes

1 A howitzer was an artillery field piece designed to fire a shell high up into the air which would then descend on its target with great accuracy, relatively close by, unlike an ordinary gun which would fire at a target some distance away, on a shallower trajectory, often unseen by the gunners. With the close proximity of positions either side of No Man's Land, howitzers, were ideal weapons for trench warfare.

2 *Field Guns in France*, by Lieutenant Colonel N. Fraser-Tytler, D.S.O., T.D. – see the bibliography for further details.

3 Lieutenant William Howard Savage is buried in Dantzig Alley British Cemetery Mametz – see Chapter Four.

4 *The Northampton Independent*, 15th July 1916.

5 *The Die-Hards In The Great War*, by E. Wyrall – see the bibliography for further details.

6 The Commonwealth War Graves Commission records that a Second Lieutenant H. R. Hudleston of the 14th Battalion The Middlesex Regiment died on 2 July 1916. He is buried in Carnoy Military Cemetery. Thus, it is likely that he was not killed on 1 July, but wounded and died of his wounds the following day in the Field Ambulance at Carnoy.

7 Some sources state that it was 7.28.

8 *The First Day on the Somme* – by M. Middlebrook – see the bibliography for further details. The author is indebted to Martin Middlebrook for allowing him to use this and other extracts from this book, which since its publication in 1972, has become the 'bible' for those interested in the events of the opening of the Battle of the Somme and its battlefields today.

9 *On the Somme* – by C. Chapman, I. Cull, C. Fox, M. McIntyre and L. Webb – see the bibliography for further details.

10 *With the 10th Essex in France*, by T.M. Banks and R.A. Chell – see the bibliography for further details.

11 Second Lieutenant Frank Gregson Rushton, of the 2/Battalion The Wiltshire Regiment, attached to 53rd Trench Mortar Battery is buried in Carnoy Military Cemetery.

12 Second Lieutenant Lancelot Hugo Saye died of his wounds on 11th July 1916 at Etaples, where he is buried today.

13 *The Norfolk Chronicle and Post*, 21st July 1916.

14 13188 Lance Corporal Robert Christopher Goulder's body was not found and identified after the war and as a consequence, he is commemorated on the Memorial to the Missing at Thiepval.

15 The bodies of Second Lieutenant John Haddon Attenborough and 3/10134 Regimental Sergeant Major Jeremiah Coe were not found and identified after the war and consequently they are both commemorated on the Memorial to the Missing at Thiepval.

16 *The 18th Division In the Great War*, by G.H.F. Nichols – see the bibliography for further details.

17 One of the officers from the 10/Essex Regiment.

18 *Bury Free Press*, (Bury St. Edmonds), 22nd July 1916.

19 *The 18th Division In the Great War*, by G.H.F. Nichols – see the bibliography for further details. G/2561 Sergeant Philip Charles (his initials were thus P.C. not P.G.) Upton from Folkestone, Kent, was awarded the Distinguished Conduct Medal for his actions in the Carnoy Craters, but never knew of his award as he was killed in action just 13 days later. Although buried at the time, his body was not found and identified after the war and as a consequence, he is commemorated on The Memorial to the Missing at Thiepval.

20 *The Official History* maintains that this incident occurred after the capture of The Loop, but Back Trench seems to be a more likely position because of the identity of the troops captured there. See also, *The First Day on the Somme*, by Martin Middlebrook, pages 186 and 187.

21 *The Surrey Advertiser and County Times*, 15th July 1916.

22 *History of The Queen's Royal Regiment, Volume VII*, by Colonel H.C. Wylly – see the bibliography for further details. Other sources spell Tortiss' name Tortise and even Tortoise.

23 The full story is related in Chapter Four.

24 As far as may be ascertained, all the officers who celebrated the victory survived the war, except Wightman. Major James Wightman, having been awarded the D.S.O. and the M.C., died of wounds received in action, still serving with the 8th East Surreys, on 9th April 1918. He is buried in Picquigny British Cemetery, France.

25 Sackville-West, (later Fourth Baron Sackville) was truly a 'fighting general' with a wealth of military experience before the Great War. He himself was wounded twice on the Somme, on 30th July and 29th October 1916 and ended the war as a Major-General on the General Staff, and became British Military Representative at Versailles – *Bloody Red Tabs* by F. Davies and G. Maddocks. See the bibliography for further details.

26 George Andrew Herdman: *The Record of a Short But Strenuous Life* by W.A. Herdman. Professor W.A. Herdman was a noted Liverpool academic and, in his son's memory, set up the George Herdman Institute at Port Erin on the Isle of Man and the George Herdman Chair of Geology at the University of Liverpool. See the bibliography for further details

27 Despite this battlefield burial, the bodies of Captain Arthur de Bels Adam, Second Lieutenant Eric Fitzbrown and Second Lieutenant George Andrew Herdman were not found and identified after the war. Consequently, they are commemorated on The Memorial to the Missing at Thiepval.

28 *The British Campaigns in Europe* by A. Conan Doyle - see the bibliography for further details.

29 This account was written in a letter to 17122 Private W. Gregory of the 18/King's in March 1939. Gregory had found Theurlein's Soldbuch (paybook) in Glatz Redoubt and taken it home as a souvenir and upon finding it 23 years later, wrote to the address inside it. The two former adversaries then began a correspondence which was only halted by the Second World War.

30 *Manchester Pals* by M. Stedman – see bibliography for details. The author is indebted to Mike Stedman for permission to use this, and other extracts, from his excellent work.

31 *The Green Howards in The Great War*, by Colonel H.C. Wylly, see the bibliography for further details.

32 *The 2nd Battalion Wiltshire Regiment A Record of their Fighting in the Great War 1914-18*, by Major W.S. Shepherd, - see the bibliography for further details.

33 *Liverpool Pals* by G. Maddocks – see the bibliography for further details. 26540 Lance Corporal, Joseph Quinn was killed in action on 30 July 1916 at the Battle of Guillemont. As his body could not be found and identified after the war, he is commemorated on the Memorial to the Missing at Thiepval.

34 Captain Ernest Charles Orford was killed in action just 30 days later during the Battle of Guillemont. His body was not found and identified after the war and as a consequence, he is commemorated on The Memorial to the Missing at Thiepval.

35 As late as the evening of 2 July, a patrol from the 20th Battalion found Bernafay Wood to be empty of troops apart from three cowering men whom they took prisoner. Despite reporting this to Divisional and Corps Headquarters, nothing was done, and the Germans were able to re-occupy it.

36 Three officers and about 100 other ranks were reported wounded in the Battalion War Diary for 1 July, which is likely to be more accurate than some, because all the officers survived. *Soldiers Died in the Great War* lists 17 men from the Battalion killed on 1/2 July, but as the Germans fiercely bombarded their former positions on 2 July, it is by no means certain that all 17, or any of them at all, were actually killed on 1 July.

37 Of the officers mentioned in this account, as far as can be ascertained, only Captain Cornelius George Tyler failed to survive the war. He was wounded the following week during the fighting for Trônes Wood, and died on 11th July. Although buried at the time, his body was not found and identified after the war and as a consequence he is commemorated on The Memorial to the Missing at Thiepval.

38 A 'Jack Johnson' was the nickname given by the British troops to a heavy calibre German shell, which, filled with gunpowder, exploded with a plume of black smoke. It was sometimes called a 'Coal Box'. Jack Johnson was an American Negro heavyweight boxer and former world champion, who was very popular at the time. British shells, more usually filled with lyddite, exploded with a burst of yellow smoke.

39 *Sixteenth : Seventeenth : Eighteenth : Nineteenth Battalions : The Manchester Regiment – A Record 1914-1918* – see the bibliography for further details.

40 Former 6254 Private Charles 'Chick' Heaton was interviewed at his home in Cheadle, Manchester, by the author on 10th April 1986. He died on 21st August 1988. 6202 Private Louis Alban was not actually a German, as he had been born in St. Michael's, Manchester, albeit of German parents. His body was not found and identified after the war and he is consequently commemorated on the Memorial to the Missing at Thiepval. Captain J. H. Worthington, commanding A Company was later wounded, but recovered to survive the war, (see Chapter Four) and Captain Wilfrith Elstob, commanding 'D' Company, survived the Somme to earn greater glory, a Military Cross, a Distinguished Service Order and a posthumous Victoria Cross defending a British redoubt, Manchester Hill, in March 1918. Private Heaton was present there too and was taken prisoner. Elstob's body was not recovered and identified after the war and he is commemorated on the Memorial to the Missing of the Fifth Army at Pozieres.

41 *The History of The Royal Scots Fusiliers (1678-1918)* by J. Buchan – see the bibliography for further details.

42 The literal French translation of Nettoyeur is 'cleaner', but the French Army used it to mean 'mopper-upper'. A lot of British Army units adopted the term in its pure form and used it in every day language.

43 The author is indebted to advanced Royal Scots Fusiliers researcher Greg Ward of Rotherham, South Yorkshire for most of the information contained in this section. Although the views expressed here are those of the author the conclusions reached lean heavily on the evidence provided by Mr. Ward.

44 Some sources state that the two were Privates Aldcroft and Dawson.

45 10805 Lance Corporal Robert Kendall and Second Lieutenant Herbert Lonsdale Atkins of the 2/Royal Scots Fusiliers, were both killed in action during the Battle of Guillemont on 30th July 1916 and neither of their bodies were found and identified after the war. Consequently, they are both commemorated on the memorial to the Missing at Thiepval.

46 *'Ich Dien' The Prince of Wales's Volunteers (South Lancashire) 1914-1934* by Captain H. Whalley-Kelly – see the bibliography for further details.

Chapter Three

TOURS OF THE OLD BATTLEFIELDS

These tours are designed to show the traveller what remains of the battlefield sites of the successful attacks of 1 July 1916 at Montauban. They are meant to be followed from left to right, from the left hand brigade of the 18th Division to the right hand brigade of the 30th Division, in exactly the same way that the 'blow by blow' accounts of the battles are outlined in the main text. They are also set out in brigade and then battalion order, so that a traveller with a particular interest in a particular unit can more easily discover where that unit fought.

Because of the differing nature of the land in the XIII Corps attack area, which often led to differing fortunes on the day, the tours are a mixture of driving or cycling and walking. For some areas there is little to see today, as the Battle of the Somme moved onwards and northwards, leaving no permanent scar on the surface after 1916. Although the area of the Somme was fought over again in 1918, none of it made its real mark on the Montauban Ridge. Today, for the most part, there is more to see and identify in the area fought over by the 30th Division, than that in the 18th.

Originally, the French government had intended to turn the whole of the Somme battleground area into a vast wooded memorial park, like the area around Verdun, but immediately after the war the British still held it whilst they were clearing the battlefields and winding down the millions of parts of war materiel still stored there. Not knowing French intentions, they had no objection to villagers and farmers returning to their former homes. As a result, Montauban, Maricourt and Carnoy were cleared by the simple expedient of filling all the shell holes and dugouts with the rubble from destroyed buildings, and eventually re-building the villages on top. The original inhabitants began to return as early as 1919 and for the most part, the village buildings were re-erected much as they had been, although all three villages were significantly smaller when the re-building was completed in the 1930s.

Montauban during the course of re-building in 1925.

When the farmers returned to agriculture – a necessity in near starving post-war France – they needed to level off the land as soon as possible so that they could begin to re-plough and the first thing they did was to fill in the old trench lines. As a result, after the passage of some 80 years, most of these have disappeared from obvious view. No agriculturalist was surprised to find that the crop yield in the early 1920s was much, much higher than it had been in 1913 – the last years that crops had been taken from the fields around Montauban. The fact that these fields had lain fallow for half a dozen years or more was responsible for this – along with the excellent natural fertiliser that human blood makes.

In an effort to convince the farmers that they should declare the bodies that they inevitably discovered in the course of their work, each of the involved governments, British, French and German offered cash inducements for the recovery of corpses in the post war years, to prevent the farmers from merely re-ploughing them back into the earth. The only problem with this, was that each government offered a different amount – the British offering the highest. Most farmers did not need such an inducement, mindful of the sacrifices made on their soil, but it was often believed at the time that if a body was discovered with no evident nationality, then it was all too easy to throw a few British Army buttons or a cap badge into the grave and then call out the (then) Imperial War Graves Commission, rather than its French or German counterparts – and thereby claim the highest amount- It is interesting to speculate how widespread was this practice and how many fallen French or German soldiers might be buried in British graves in British cemeteries under the title 'An Unknown Soldier', as a consequence.

This not withstanding, it is a curious facet of the British character that we rarely erect monuments on Great War battlefield sites where great victories have been achieved, only where great losses have occurred. Even at the battlefield site of Waterloo, the only British memorials commemorate soldiers killed in the battle, not the victory itself. Thus, although the XIII Corps area was probably the most successful and victorious area on 1 July 1916, there are few major post-war memorials on it. Consequently, there are few navigable roads across the old farmland. Similarly, all the war cemeteries in the area are concentration ones, mostly completed after the Armistice and are built on the sides of roads that existed before the war. There were other, smaller battlefield cemeteries in existence during the fighting, but these were moved after the war was over.[1]

As a result, even if one is certain of the exact location of a trench, dugout or redoubt, there is often little to see today on most of the battlefield sites. As they are almost exclusively on private land, access is only from existing roads and tractor/cart tracks. So long as there is **not** a crop in a field, however, most farmers will respond well to a polite request to visit a particular location. Even though few farmers on the Somme speak English, they are, by now, used to *'mad'* English visitors.

One very important thing to bear in mind when studying the battlefields, however, is that there is always unexploded ammunition and ordnance literally lying around. This is not only because the farmers of today use deeper ploughing methods which bring hitherto undiscovered debris to the surface, but also because of the high proportion of duds fired by both sides in the run up to the Somme battle and then during the battle itself. It is estimated that well over a million shells were fired by the British alone *in the week before the battle started*, so one can easily imagine how many more were fired in total by both sides by the time the battle reached its weary conclusion in November 1916. Most of those that did not explode were of faulty construction, which is hardly surprising when one appreciates the complexity of the workings of a shrapnel shell, which carried a time and percussion fuze. This type was timed to explode in the air to cause maximum damage to infantry and cavalry but if the timing unit failed, then it was meant to explode on impact with the ground.

However, the problem with this common type could be two-fold. None of the warring nations before the war started really anticipated the gigantic need there would be for literally millions of shells, and the existing specialist ordnance factories were soon swamped with orders they could never fulfil. The only answer was to tender out shell making to any engineering company that believed it could handle the work. The result was a similar mixture on both sides – some firms coped very well and made shells to a high quality, whilst others, who had maybe been making sewing machines or lawn mowers a year earlier, certainly did not. Add to this the fact that the fuzes used on most shrapnel shells were very complex anyway (mostly in the Type 80 series in the British Army and the Dopp. Z series in the German), it is not surprising that they often failed to detonate.

On the other hand, many shells fired during the 'mud' phase of the Battle of the Somme, including shrapnel shells whose timer units failed and high explosive ones (which were supposed to detonate on impact), failed to explode simply because they sank into the softened

'The Iron Harvest.' Unexploded shells in the sunken road just outside Montauban.

ground and did not achieve sufficient concussion to detonate their percussion units. Thus, if discovered today, they may well be in the same lethal state as when they were fired – or even *more* so. Often, the passage of time has made them more dangerous, as the explosive inside them is now more unstable than when they were first issued from the ordnance factories. Some travellers forget that these instruments of war were designed and meant to kill and maybe only failed to explode because they were abandoned at the time – not because they were faulty.

If ordnance, often known as 'The Iron Harvest', is on the corner of a field or at a cross-roads, it has been found by a farmer and deliberately left there for collection and disposal by the French Army – which happens at regular intervals throughout the year. Farmers generally know what they have found and if they have left anything alone, then logically so should a traveller. Finding battlefield debris in an open field is often even more dangerous, as you might be the first person to see it for over 80 years. The simple rule is to leave everything which is lying around well alone – if you are desperate for a souvenir, there are plenty of places where you can purchase safe, deactivated ones.

Ridiculously, British Type 80 fuzes were based upon a design perfected and patented by the German armaments giant Friedrich Krupp and before the war, the British government had agreed to pay a royalty to Krupp for every fuze it made under licence. After the war, in the 1920s, Krupp successfully sued the British government in the international court for non-payment of royalties on fuzes used during the war – the vast proportion of them fired at German subjects.

The nature of the land you will cross will obviously vary depending on the time of year that a visit is made, so it is well to bear this in mind before setting out on any walk. Apart from this guide, other useful things for a traveller to take would be a compass, a copy of the French IGN serie bleu map 1:25,000 scale, 2408 est, a copy of the Commonwealth War Graves Commission, Michelin 1:200,000 map No. 52, with overprinted cemetery details, appropriate clothes/footwear and copious amounts of drink in hot weather. Whilst walking, also, it might be useful to make the rough calculation that one average pace is roughly equal to one yard. The tours of the XIII Corps area are:

Tour One – General Circuit of the 18th and 30th Division Attack Area.
Tour Two – 18th Division – 54 Brigade Attack Area.
Tour Three– 18th Division – 53 and 55 Brigade Attack Area.
Tour Four – 18th Division – 55 Brigade Attack Area.
Tour Five – 30th Division – 21 and 90 Brigade Attack Area.
Tour Six – 30th Division – 21, 90 and 89 Brigade Attack Area.
Tour Seven– 30th Division – Across Caterpillar Valley.

TOUR ONE

A General Circuit of the 18th and 30th Division Attack Areas

Tour One is designed to introduce the battlefield traveller to the area fought over and captured by the 18th and 30th Divisions on 1 July 1916. Ideally a car should be used, although it is quite possible to complete the tour by bicycle. Without stopping, and driving at a steady 30 m.p.h., (45 k.p.h.) it should take approximately 16 minutes, covering eight miles, although it is recommended that travellers do stop frequently at points of interest.

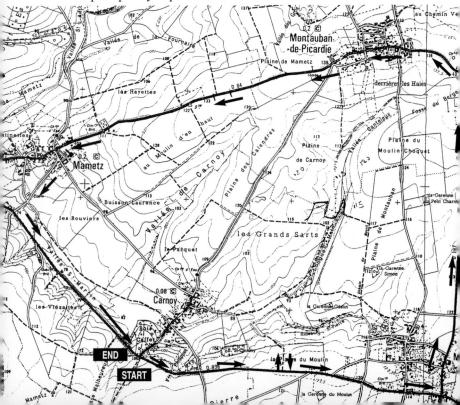

TALUS BOISE

CARNOY MILITARY CEMETERY

CAFTET WOOD

ALBERT TO PERONNE RD

The battlefield from Carnoy looking towards Longueval. On the left is the site of Minden Post, next to Caftet Wood. Beyond the wood is Carnoy Military Cemetery, burial place of Captain W P Nevill. In the centre is Talus Boisé and the road is the Albert to Péronne Road – the D938.

The tour begins at the junction of the D 938 Albert to Péronne road and the D254 Carnoy to Montauban road, at the corner of what is called Bois Caffet on modern maps but was known to the British as Caftet Wood. It is worth noting, however, before starting Tour One, that about 350 yards back on the north side of the D 938 towards Mametz, on the right hand side of the road, was the site of Minden Post, where there was a dressing station and headquarters throughout the Somme battle. It was there that scenes shown in the famous Battle of the Somme film were taken by official cameramen Malins and Macdowall, of wounded British and Germans being brought in and treated. The edge of Minden Post marked the divisional boundary between the XV and XII Corps and it is here that our tour proper begins.

It was in Caftet Wood that 54 Brigade sheltered on the night of 30 June 1916 before going up the line for the attack the following morning, and the wood is much the same size and shape now as it was then. Begin driving along the D. 938 in the direction of Maricourt and on the left side of the road Carnoy comes into view through a dip in the road. Just after this, Carnoy Military Cemetery is seen in a hollow, where amongst other dead of the 1st July attack is buried Captain W.P. Nevill of the footballs fame.[1] The turning for the cemetery is about 100 yards further down the road on the left, signposted Carnoy Military Cemetery on the familiar green Commonwealth War Graves Commission signpost.

As you continue along the main road you soon get a perfect view of Montauban sitting on top of the ridge and it is immediately obvious

Carnoy Military Cemetery.

why the Germans fortified it for defence. At this point you are looking up towards where 21, 90 and 89 Brigades made their successful assault and you can clearly see the woods which played a part in this. Pointing upwards towards Montauban like a long finger is Talus Boisé, now called La Longue Haie and next to it and to the right is Machine Gun Wood (La Garenne Simon) and further over is Germans Wood (La Garenne Petit Charme). On the skyline to the right of Montauban and appearing, from this position, to blend into one, are Bernafay Wood (Bois Bernafay) and Trônes Wood (Bois des Troncs). Beyond Trônes Wood you can see the steeple of the church at Guillemont.

Half a mile along the road after the Carnoy Cemetery turning, a track leads off to the left. It is worth while stopping here for two reasons. The first is that this is the rough location of the southern boundary between the 18th and 30th Divisions and the second is that the track leads down from the Maricourt Ridge towards the southern end of Talus Boisé. Follow the track down the slope and where it forks, take the right fork for a few yards. Stretching away from you, you now have a perfect view of the battleground from the British lines up to

An army chaplain tending a soldier's grave, Carnoy Valley, July 1916 – now Carnoy Military Cemetery.

Montauban itself. Immediately below you and to the right is Oxford Copse, called Rideau St. Pierre on modern maps and, beyond that, Cambridge Copse, now called la Garenne Gustin. Both Oxford and Cambridge Copses sheltered troops of the 2/Wiltshires of 21 Brigade and some of 90 Brigade, awaiting their turn to advance in the second wave on the early morning of 1 July.

Returning to the main road, as you continue along the D 939, the outskirts of Maricourt are reached after about half a mile and on the left is *Péronne Road Cemetery*, where a lot of the dead of 1 July and later battles are buried. Proceed along the road and, ignoring the first cross-roads, signposted to Maricourt, turn left at the next, on to the D 197, signposted to Longueval. A brewery originally stood on the north-eastern corner of this road and its junction with the D 938, to be replaced during the war by a military cemetery originally known as *Maricourt Military Cemetery*. The bodies from this cemetery were moved after the Armistice to *Cerisy-Gailly Military Cemetery*, on the south bank of the Somme river.[1]

Drive up the D 197 in the direction of Longueval and you will notice that the road begins to rise slightly up towards Montauban and on the right, after about a quarter of a mile, you will see Maricourt Wood. Originally, Maricourt Château stood on the left of the road, just as the buildings peter out, and it was here that the 19/King's sheltered on the morning and early afternoon of 1 July before going up the line as carriers for the Brigade. As you draw level with the tip of the wood, you are at the point of the British front line trench held by the 17/King's and its start line for the attack. The trackway across the top of the wood is still called Chemin des Anglais (Route of the English), today. At this point, the road follows the demarcation line between the British and French armies but just before you reach Germans Wood, (known to the Germans as Schrapnell Wald), about half a mile on the left, the line veers off to the right.

By now you have crossed No Man's Land and the German front and support line trenches, (Favière Trench and Favière Alley) and about a quarter of a mile further on, you are on the site of Dublin Trench. At this point, if you turn to the left to where the ground rises slightly, you are looking at what used to be Glatz Redoubt and if you turn to the right, and look in the direction of the wood (Favière Wood, or Bayern Wald, to the Germans), you will see the site of the German Dublin Redoubt, captured by the French 153e R.I. at 8.30 am on that first day of the battle. Dublin Alley, a German communication trench which connected Favière Alley with the Briqueterie, ran parallel and to the right of the road, bisecting Dublin Trench. As you look up the slope of the road at this point, Montauban is very clear on your left and Bernafay Wood, is on the horizon with Trônes Wood to its right. On a clear day you can make out Delville Wood beyond that.

Just before you reach the cross-roads below Bernafay Wood, there is a clump of trees, bushes and unploughed land on the left hand side of the road. This is the site of the so-called Briqueterie captured at approximately 12.30 pm by the 20/King's. In point of fact, before the war the Briqueterie stood on the right hand side of the road and on the left, where the ruins are today, stood a sugar beet works, but on British Army wartime maps, both sides of the road were labelled Briqueterie. The ruins are now dangerous and fenced off and should not be approached.

Once the cross-roads is reached, take the left fork to Montauban itself and entering, the village, note the memorial to the Liverpool and Manchester Pals on the left of the road at the next cross-roads. This memorial commemorates the capture of the village by men of the 30th Division on 1 July – the most successful victory of the day anywhere on the Somme battle front – and was only erected as recently as 1994.[1] Continue along the road, the D 64,

The station at Montauban before the war.

Montauban with the end of Bernafay Wood on the right where Montauban Railway Station once stood. The remains of the Briqueterie, captured by the 20th KLR are in the centre

MONTAUBAN

BERNAFAY WOOD

BRIQUETERIE

OLD RAILWAY STATION SITE

Interior of Montauban church in 1915.

passing the church – L 'Eglise de St. Giles, on your right. Nothing remains of the original village today and in common with most villages on the Somme it was built afresh in the 1920s, the rubble from the original buildings being used to fill in the dugouts, trenches and shell holes.

The tour continues through the village and out the other side, past the road junction on the left, signposted to Carnoy. The first thing to note just after this junction, on the right side of the road, is a grey granite memorial cross with an inscription which commemorates Capitaine de Monclin and men of the 69e R.I. who died there in the unsuccessful attempt to recapture Montauban on 28 September 1914.[1] This cross is on the site of the village windmill which was destroyed in the fighting and never rebuilt after the war. As one might expect from the site of a windmill, this spot is slightly higher than the rest of the land, (although the Great War flattened most of its original

Montauban today.

The bells from the church of St Giles, Montauban, after the village was captured

high position) and is an excellent place to stop, as from here you can see right across Caterpillar Valley. The wood on your left is Mametz Wood and on its left, on the skyline, the Memorial to the Missing at Thiepval can be seen. Right in front of you are the Bazentin Woods and perversely, then, as now, Bazentin le Petit Wood is larger than Bazentin le Grand, although on modern maps they are called Bois Bazentin and Bois de la Perreuse respectively. Also on the skyline near the Bazentin Woods, you can see the red and white French Army radio mast which is just behind the Tank Corps Memorial near Pozières, on the D 929 Albert to Bapaume Road.

Down below on the floor of the valley and slightly to the left, is Caterpillar Wood itself, obviously thus named by the British, because of its shape, but called Bois des Montagnes by the French. In 1916 a stream ran alongside it through the valley floor, but this has long since

Caterpillar Valley and Wood.

gone. The valley is called La Vallée des Gros Cerisiers, on modern maps. On the right hand side of the ridge, on the skyline, you can see Delville Wood. Parallel with the road, just inside Caterpillar Valley and running for the next three-quarters of a mile towards the village of Mametz, was Montauban Alley, the furthest point reached by troops of the 18th and 30th Divisions on that terrible day.

About three hundred yards further down the road on the right, there used to stand a small wood named Orchard Copse, captured by the 7/Queens at 2 pm on 1 July 1916 and now no longer in existence and, just beyond this, on the left, was the position known as The Twins, captured by the 7/Buffs just after noon. For the battlefield traveller of today, however, eager to discover the sites of struggle, the near-unique 1st July victories in this area have not been helpful. Once the Somme battle moved onwards from the Montauban Ridge towards the desperate struggle for the woods, no redoubts or trenches or even memorials were left behind to show where the old fighting had been, as the land was returned to the plough. In other areas of the Somme or the Ypres Salient, the land was so badly knocked around through constant fighting over a long period of time that the scars of strife will be there for many years to come.

SITE OF THE
POMMIERS REDOUBT

DANTZIG ALLEY CEMETERY

← MAMETZ TO MONTAUBAN RD →

The 18th Division battlefield from the German positions. The Mametz to Montauban road cuts through the centre of the photograph with Dantzig alley Cemetery on the right. The remains of the Pommiers Redoubt can be clearly seen to the left of the centre. Carnoy is in the background and the fighting took place in between.

There are one or two reference points on the road, however, to show where some of the more outstanding features of the fighting of 1 July 1916 took place. About a quarter of a mile further down the road on the left, is a line of trees, planted as a wind break. Just opposite the last of these, on the right hand side of the road, a track goes down into Caterpillar Valley. This track is on the advance line of the 6/Royal Berkshires as they crossed the road to reach Montauban Alley at that point, having fought up Loop Trench from The Loop itself. This fortified position was about a quarter of a mile to the left, down the slope through where the trees are today. About a quarter of a mile further along the D 64, a staggered track crosses the road left and right and this is roughly where Maple Trench met the road from The Loop and where men from the 7/Bedfords and the 10/Essex met.

About a quarter of a mile further down the road on the left, on a slight rise, is the site of Pommiers Redoubt. This slight rise in the ground is the only clue today of the position of the fortifications fought over so valiantly and captured by the 7/Bedfords, the 11/Royal Fusiliers and the 6/Northamptons. Just down the road towards Mametz marks the eastern edge of the 18th Divisonal boundary and just after this you reach Dantzig Alley Cemetery on the right. Although this cemetery is not within XIII Corps attack area on the first day of the Somme battle, many of its dead are buried there. If, however, you cross the road opposite the gate to the cemetery and look to the left up the slight slope in the field, you can see the remains of Danzig Alley Trench, which gave the cemetery its name. This trench became Maple

Dantzig Alley Cemetery.

Trench as it moved into XIII Corps' area, some quarter of a mile away.

To make a complete circuit of the 18th and 30th Divisional attack areas, it is now necessary to enter, albeit briefly, into XV Corps' area. Keeping on the D 64, drive into the village of Mametz itself and at the first cross-roads, with the village war memorial and the memorial to the Manchester Regiment on your right, turn left in the direction of Carnoy. Instead of going to Carnoy, however, take the right hand fork of the road, signposted Vers D 938, and actually called Rue de L'Atre. This road soon takes you past the civilian Mametz Cemetery, site of the German machine-gun which did so much damage to the 2/Devons on 1st July and down to the main road with the old railway station on the right.[2] Turn left here and drive once more on the D 938, towards Carnoy. On the way, you will pass Mansell Copse and Devonshire Cemetery on the high ground on your right and the circular Gordon Cemetery on your left, before passing the site of Minden Post and arriving once more at the cross-roads and Caftet Wood. You have now driven a complete circuit of XIII Corps' area on 1 July 1916 and it is time to explore each part of the battlefield in more detail.

TOUR TWO

18th Division - 54 Brigade Attack Area

Tour Two covers the area fought over and captured by 54 Brigade of the 18th Division. Because of the high density of arable land covering the former 18th Divisional attack area, it is only possible to use tractor and cart tracks to tour it and in any case it is only possible to see where prominent battlefield positions used to be, as the plough has claimed the whole area back since 1918. As a result, Tour Two may *only* be undertaken on foot. The return journey should take about 45 minutes, walking at a steady pace.

The tour begins in Mametz at the cross-roads marked Vers D 938, Rue de L'Atre, as in Tour One. This time, however, instead of turning off towards the D 938, keep on the road to Carnoy. After about three hundred yards, there is a track on the left, which leads up the slope. Ignore this and drive or walk for another 200 yards until you come to another track on the left. Stop here, and if you are in a car, park it here, being careful to allow space for agricultural vehicles to pass. This point roughly marks the boundary between the 7th Division and the 18th on 1 July 1916, but at this point you are more or less on the start line of

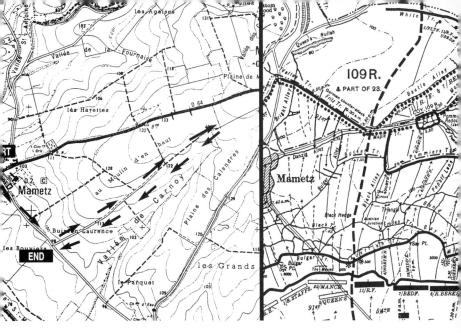

the 22/Manchesters of 91 Brigade, 7th Division. It helps, at this stage, if you have a compass with you for you will see that the track bears north east up the slope. The attack of 1st July was made almost exactly from south to north and once you have found north with the aid of the compass, it gives you your bearings as you look up the slope.

Once you start to walk up the track, although there are no remains of trench or earthworks to see, it is possible to work out where they would have been. After a few yards you are crossing the front line German trench, named Austrian Trench and assaulted on that morning by men of the 11/Royal Fusiliers. Immediately north of you, (turn slightly to the left) would have been Emden Trench and a quarter of a

The main battlefield area of the 18 Division. Mametz is to the right and Dantzig Alley Cemetery is on the Mametz to Montauban road. The remains of the Pommiers Redoubt can be seen on the bend in the road.

SITE OF THE
POMMIERS REDOUBT

DANTZIG ALLEY CEMETERY

MAMETZ

mile away on the ridge, the point of Pommiers Trench, guarding Pommiers Redoubt. After 200 yards you are now in the sector attacked by the 7/Bedfords and as No Man's Land was wider here, you are still only just behind the old German front line. Another 200 yards takes you into the area assaulted by the 8/Norfolks and immediately behind you now is the position known as Bay Point. You will have noticed by now that the ground is becoming increasingly steep and as you look up the slope you will appreciate how well the German engineers had sited their positions and how difficult it must have been for the men of the Eastern Division to dislodge them.

Continuing up the track for another 400 yards, (approximately fifteen minutes walking time, to allow for the slope and the rough going), you are crossing near the junction of Popoff Lane and Bund Support trenches and immediately north of you would have been Pommiers Trench on the high ground and beyond it, on the top of the ridge, just in front of the main road, which you can not see from this position, Pommiers Redoubt. Another four hundred yards further on, as you reach the rough position where Pommiers Trench would have been, over to the left would have been The Loop at the head of Carnoy Valley. This is marked by a section of uneven ground which has never since totally accepted the plough. Just after this, the track peters out and becomes a hedge for about fifty yards. From here Loop Trench went north to the Mametz to Montauban Road and, from the top end of the hedge, it is possible to get your bearings by looking at Montauban itself over to the right. A line of trees to your left is actually on the D 64 main road, about half a mile outside the village, on the road to Mametz. These are the same trees, planted as a wind break, that are mentioned in Tour One and mark the spot where the 6/Royal Berkshires crossed the road.

The top of the hedge is the furthest point you can reach on the trackway and you must now re-trace your steps down to the Mametz to Carnoy road once more, this time appreciating the perspective that the Germans would have had as they looked down on their British attackers. It is also worth noting as you get to the bottom of the track, that immediately in front of you is the Maricourt Ridge, with the D 938

Looking across Carnoy Valley towards the area of the 54 Brigade attack. The line of hedges is just beyond the position known as The Loop and the trees on the left are actually on the Mametz to Montauban road.

THE LOOP

Albert to Péronne Road running along its top. It was behind the road here, all along the reverse slope of the ridge, that British Artillery batteries were sited, virtually impregnable to German retaliatory fire.

TOUR THREE

18th Division – 53 and 55 Brigade Attack Area

Tour Three covers the area fought over and captured by 53 and 55 Brigades of the 18th Division. For the same reasons as for Tour Two, it is only possible to use a tractor/cart track to tour it, as the rest of the fields of the former battlefield sites are private farmland. Like Tour Two, Tour Three may *only* be undertaken on foot and it is also a good idea, once more, to take a compass with you.

The tour begins where Tour Two ended, at the bottom of the track on

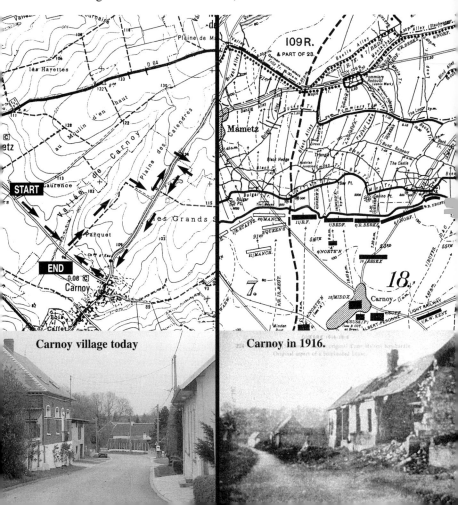

Carnoy village today

Carnoy in 1916.

the road which connects Mametz with Carnoy and facing the direction of Carnoy immediately ahead of you - the church steeple is clearly visible. Walk or drive half a mile along the road until you come to another track on the left side of the road. If driving, leave your car at the foot of the track, being careful to allow space for agricultural vehicles to pass, and begin to walk up it. Although the surface is metalled at first, after about thirty yards this solid surface peters out and becomes an earth track, not suitable for cars – even in summer.

Remembering, once more that the attack of 1st July was mounted northwards from the road, you must walk for half a mile up the track before you come to the start line of 1 July. On a slight rise, it was from here on your left that the 7/Bedfords of 54 Brigade left their front line and on your right, where the 6/Royal Berkshires of 53, went over the top. As the whole area has been ploughed and re-ploughed many times since 1918, the land is fairly featureless, but about two hundred yards further on, you are able to identify your exact position as the track suddenly veers to the left and then back to the right. This is the exact spot of Casino Point, where the mine was exploded late, showering debris on the attacking waves of the Brigade. It shows you exactly the position of the old German front line, where Bay Trench joined up with Mine Trench to form the salient, jutting out into No Man's Land. Although the Casino Point mine crater has long since been filled in, you can nevertheless see a slight depression in the ground on the left, where the earth is still settling.

About two hundred yards further on, the track takes a 90 degree bend to the right, which you have to follow. It is obvious that you are in the region of the German front line because of the height of the ground here. Before making the turn, however, look to the north across Carnoy Valley and directly ahead of you on the top of the ridge was the site of Pommiers Redoubt, with all the defensive and communication trenches before it. Montauban is over to the right. The track now takes you slightly south east, but after about two hundred yards, if you look north again, up towards the ridge, you will see where The Castle used to be. You have now crossed back into No Man's Land and are in the area of the 8/Norfolks attack. After another two hundred yards, you once again reach the main Carnoy to Montauban road, – the surface of the track is, once again, metalled for the last thirty yards or so.

Turn left onto the main road and walk up the slope in the direction of Montauban for about another 200 yards. As you are walking you will notice a small copse on the eastern side of the road and as you get closer you will notice something unusual about it – you are only seeing

SITE OF
CRATER

The left swerve of the track marks the original location of the Casino Point Mine Crater and the hedge on the left of the skyline is just beyond the position known as The Loop.

the tops of trees and not the trunks or the bottoms. The reason for this soon becomes obvious – the bottoms of the trees are in a large hollow – and you are looking at all that remains of the Carnoy Crater Field today. The hollow is formed from several overlapping craters now used as a dumping ground for modern debris – mainly agricultural. Because there is a small trackway leading to the hollow, however, you are able to walk right around it and work out not only the exact attack position of the 7/Buffs, of 55 Brigade, but also the defensive positions of 6. Bayerisches Reserve Infanterie–Regiment. As you would expect, the German side of the crater looks down on that of the British, but from that side, you are easily able to see just how close the two sides were on that fateful day and exactly why No Man's Land was so narrow at that point. On returning to the main road you will see that very little remains of the crater field on the western side of the road, but if you climb the bank there you can still detect slight depressions in the ground where it is still settling, like the Casino Point crater. Whilst on top of the bank you have a perfect view up towards Montauban, where the various trenches leading up to Montauban Ridge and the main Mametz to Montauban road once stood, but nothing now remains of them after eighty years of arable use.

At this point, you have a choice, depending on whether or not you used a car. If you did not, you can now, if you wish, follow Tour Four. If you did, however, either simply re-trace your steps, or walk down the road to Carnoy and just before the main part of the village, turn right where it is signposted to Mametz, and pick up your vehicle. Whichever return route you take, the overall distance is about two miles, which should take no more than 45 minutes to walk, perhaps a little less if your return route is on the road.

All that remains of the crater field to the right of the Carnoy to Montauban road – the tops of the trees.

TOUR FOUR

18th Division – 55 Brigade Attack Area

Tour Four explores the area fought over and captured by 53 and 55 Brigades of the 18th Division. Once again, apart from what can be seen from the Carnoy to Montauban road, it is virtually all across a tractor/cart track. Thus, like Tours Two and Three it may *only* be undertaken on foot. Once again, a compass is very useful.

The tour begins on the Carnoy to Montauban road, just opposite where the track meets the road at the end of Tour Three and up the road by about eighty yards. Here you will find a track to the right of the road, which looks directly across towards Talus Boisé and crosses what is called Les Grand Sarts on modern French maps. Where this track begins is just in front of the old German front line, known at this point as Breslau Trench. Some 200 yards down the track is the site of the British attack trenches of the 8/Norfolks of 53 Brigade and the 7/Buffs of 55. At this point, the British front line jutted forward, forming a

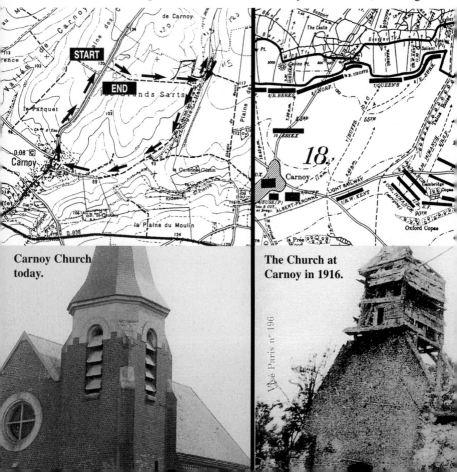

Carnoy Church today.

The Church at Carnoy in 1916.

small salient, up against the crater field, where No Man's Land was virtually nothing but the craters themselves. After you have covered about a mile, you are more or less half way to Talus Boisé and you are back behind the British front line, facing the area occupied by the 7/Queens before the attack on 1 July. From here, you get a perfect view of Montauban directly north-east of you on the ridge. This is the view that the men from Guildford would have seen as they left their trenches that morning, although Allied artillery had, by then, all but reduced the village to rubble.

A further 400 yards further down the track puts you behind the start line of the 8/East Surreys on that dreadful morning. The front line trenches at this point veered up and forward to form another salient which jutted upwards beyond the tip of Talus Boisé, as the contour of the land formed a small valley as it fell down towards the wood. The start line of the East Surreys was on one piece of high ground and the German front line at Breslau Point was on another, with the small valley in between. Thus the East Surreys had to cross the valley and attack up towards Breslau Trench and Breslau Point, where the German front line also took a change of direction to maintain the domination of the high ground at that point. One can appreciate the task of Captain Nevill's 'footballers' here, as the distance across No Man's Land suddenly changed from 200 yards at Breslau Point to nearly 400 yards. Furthermore, the salient at Breslau Point meant that the attackers could be fired on from ahead and from the left. One can get a better view of this area, from the German perspective, in Tour Five.

Having studied the advance of 1 July from the track, now follow it down to where it ends, near the north-western edge of Talus Boisé. It is worth walking alongside the wood to its tip if only to show you that the German positions in front of Montauban were completely hidden from the attackers at this point, until they managed to crest the hill and were then in full view of the machine-gunners of 6. Bayerisches Reserve Infanterie-Regiment, firing not only from Breslau Point, but also from The Warren, a quarter of a mile to the rear.

Once at the tip of the wood, look upwards to Montauban, which is due north, but appears to be to the left. Across the field in front of you

The remains of the old railway embankment on the right, leading to the tip of Talus Boise, front line on 1 July 1916.

NT LINE

TALUS BOISE

Montauban from the British start line of the 8 East Surreys. Breslau Point is in the centre of the photograph and Captain Nevill's footballs were kicked across the hollows just in front.

are the remains of the embankment, built pre-war to carry the Albert to Péronne light railway, which was later to give Train Alley its name. Beyond that, below Montauban, is the ground fought over by the men of 21 and 90 Brigades as they took the village from its Bavarian defenders.

From the tip of the wood, retrace your steps past a modern hunting lodge to where you came off the track. At this stage, depending on time and inclination, you can either return to the Carnoy to Montauban road in reverse of the way you have come, or simply carry on down the side of the wood, which eventually meets a track which then takes you to the centre of Carnoy village. You can then either walk back up the Mametz to Carnoy road or to your starting point on the Carnoy to Montauban road to your car, in whichever place you have left it.

The 'there and back' trip across Les Grand Sarts is approximately two miles long and without stopping, should take about an hour to walk, bearing in mind the unevenness of the ground. If you continue on down the edge of Talus Boisé to Carnoy, however, it is about two and a half miles back to whatever was your staring point and should take about an hour and a quarter as the going is easier, once more without stopping, although in both tours, there are ample enough sights to arrest the attention and hold the interest.

TOUR FIVE

30th Division – 21 and 90 Brigade Attack Area

Tour Five covers the area fought over and captured by 21 and 90 Brigades of the 30th Division, but unlike the other tours, the battleground is seen from the German perspective – i.e. looking down from Montauban to where the British attackers struggled up the slope towards the village. It may only be undertaken on foot.

It begins at the Liverpool and Manchester Pals Memorial in

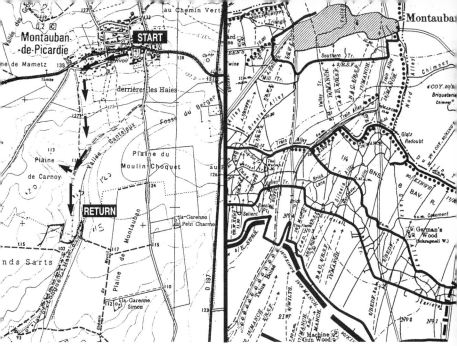

Montauban. Facing the direction of Mametz, drive or walk through the village on the main D 64 road. Just as you are leaving the village, there is a left turning towards Carnoy. Take this turning and turn again immediately to the left and if driving, park the car. You are now on the outskirts of the village itself which was more built up before the Great War; immediately opposite you is a signpost for Rue Neuve, which leads down the slope towards Railway Valley. Take this turning and you are now seeing the land as the Germans would have seen it before and during the attack of 1 July 1916.

The battleground of the 30th Division attack, from Maricourt. The road which bisects the centre of the photograph leads to Montauban and the severe bend in it marks the position of the front line of the 17 KLR. To the left is Machine Gun Wood and to the right is Germans Wood. The road to the right marks the division of the British and French Armies. Maricourt Wood is to the right of the road.

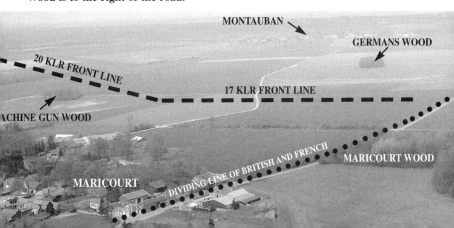

Talus Boisé taken from the German position known as Breslau Point. On the left of the photograph is the remains of the embankment which carried the light railway and the hollow in the middle is where the 8 East Surreys kicked their footballs. Their start line is the mound on the right.

The road is metalled at this stage and gradually climbs down the slope. The tip of Talus Boisé, can clearly be seen at bottom right and has altered little since 1916. The road and the wood marked the boundaries of the 18th and 30th Divisions on 1 July and the tip of this wood was the start line of the attack and facing north, the 8/East Surreys of 55 Brigade were on the left and the 18/King's of 21 Brigade, on the right. Beyond the King's was the 19/Manchesters. The defending troops were from 6. Bayerisches Reserve Infanterie-Regiment. Also visible from this point is the embankment that carried the old light railway which ran from Longueval through the Montauban battlefield through Carnoy and Albert and Péronne.

As you leave Montauban itself, you come into the open and across the valley to the left you can see Maricourt Wood and Maricourt itself. Maricourt Ridge, which bears the D 938 Albert to Péronne road, is on the skyline. After a quarter of a mile the road you are on bisects Southern Trench, where it jutted out in a salient pointing down the slope. This trench was the German third line and was important because it was the final defensive trench around the southern part of Montauban. In the event, however, the Germans abandoned it without a serious fight. After another 100 yards, the road crosses the junction between Mill Trench and Breslau Alley. Breslau Alley was a communication trench which linked Southern Trench with Train Alley, in the German reserve line.

As the metalled road begins to level out, if you concentrate on looking left, a line of trees can be seen below a low hill. This is the bottom edge of Glatz Redoubt and the tree line marks the entrances to the original German dugouts on the reverse slope of the redoubt. This made them virtually immune to British shelling before 1 July, but once Montauban had fallen and they had been captured by the 30th Division, they became very vulnerable, as they then faced the German guns on the high ground around Guillemont, which had their exact map co-ordinates accurately marked.

As you get to the very bottom of the metalled road, there is a gap which leads into the farmer's field and the road ends. This is the point where Train Alley bisected the embankment and you are standing on the old German reserve line. Train Alley was so-called by the British because it roughly followed the line of the light railway and formed a natural defensive position. From this point on both the right and left you can clearly see the remains of the old light railway embankment. On the left, it goes across the old battleground behind Glatz Redoubt, up towards Bernafay and Trônes Woods and on the right you can see it snake down and around the edge of Talus Boisé and off in the distance in the direction of Carnoy.

If you make the effort to climb on what remains of the old railway embankment, you can continue to walk down towards Talus Boisé. After about fifty yards, look immediately to your right and at this point, about 400 yards away on a slight rise, was the German fortified position known as The Warren, which caused so much trouble to the 18/King's and the 16/Manchesters. As you continue to walk down the embankment the land either side dips slightly and you are crossing Valley Trench which was the German front line at this point. It jutted backwards to form a reverse salient here, so that the Germans could make the most of the limited high ground available to them. Similarly, if you look down towards Talus Boisé from this position, you can see the little valley which led to its tip and where the British lines also formed a reverse salient, for similar reasons.

Once you have walked half way along the length of the embankment, the land on your right begins to rise once more to the German front line at Breslau Point and Breslau Trench. On top of the rise a small valley marks No Man's Land and the high ground either side of the British and German positions. It was here that the 8/East Surreys made their attack and where the famous footballs were kicked across No-Mans Land. Unfortunately, unless you visit the area when there are no crops in the field, access to this spot is private and forbidden. Sometimes, however, the farmer has repeatedly used the same spot to drive up and down the hill to avoid spoiling his crops and

Looking towards Montauban at the junction of Train Alley; on the right are the remains of the old railway embankment.

EMBANKMENT

where his tractor tyres have flattened the earth, it is possible to walk up and crest the ridge. From the top, not only can you see the East Surrey's and German positions but you have a perfect view of Montauban way up on the ridge. It is also possible at this point, if you turn to your left, to see the copse in the crater field, (see Tour Three), more or less on the side of the Carnoy to Montauban road.

Returning down the hill, if you walk another hundred yards or so, the embankment peters out in a field, tantalisingly close to Talus Boisé. If you then retrace your steps up the embankment and back up the slope, you gain an impression of what the attackers of 21 and 90 Brigades would have seen as they stormed forward to take the village. Montauban is clearly visible on the high ground, smaller than it was in 1916, but nevertheless still commanding the ridge today.

The return tour is approximately two miles in distance and without seriously stopping to browse for any length of time, should take you about an hour to complete.

TOUR SIX

30th Division – 21, 90 and 89 Brigade Attack Area

Tour Six covers the area fought over and captured by 21, 89 and 90 Brigades of the 30th Division on 1 July 1916. It is designed to be undertaken by car or bicycle and without stopping and driving at a steady 30 m.p.h., (45 k.p.h.) it should take approximately eight minutes, covering four miles. Once more, however, it is recommended that travellers do stop frequently at points of interest.

The interior of Maricourt Church in 1916.

The tour begins on the D 938 in Maricourt at the first junction past Péronne Road Military Cemetery, with a left turn, leading to Montauban. The road is named Rue des Forges and at the first cross-roads, it becomes Rue du 45e R.I. Septembre 1914, which commemorates the part played by that unit in the successful defence of the village.[3] On the right of the road is Maricourt Church – L'Eglise du Notre Dame du Mont Carmel and it is worth noting war debris immediately opposite it, against the wall of the farm there. Two types of Great War 'vintage' dug-out roof

134

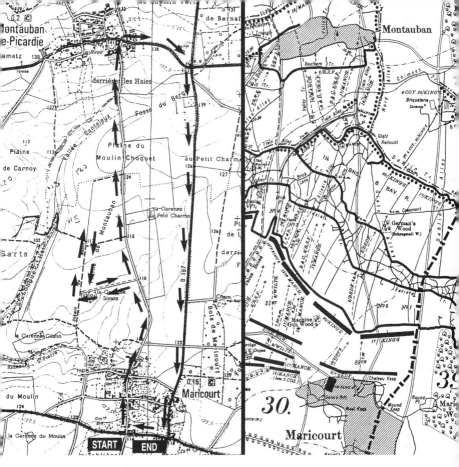

START END

supports are stacked there – some British 'wriggly tin', is on the left, much narrower and thinner than its German 'elephant iron' counterpart which is on the right, and thicker and heavier. If nothing else, the two different types emphasise the different attitudes of the warring nations to trench building. The Germans assumed that they were there to stay until they either advanced further or were ousted and thus made their trench conditions as safe and as permanent as possible. The British Army, on the other hand, assumed that any trench opposing the enemy was of a temporary nature, held only until a victorious advance became a reality and therefore did not encourage its troops to think of it as

The remains of the light railway embankment looking towards the Glatz Redoubt and Bernafay and Trônes Wood on the skyline. Photograph taken from Breslau Point. Montauban is on the skyline on the left.

MONTAUBAN   GLATZ REDOUBT   BERNAFAY WOOD   TRONES WOOD anything else but a temporary structure.

Maricourt was the forming up point for the attack of 89 Brigade, and the junction between the British and French Armies. Once you have driven out of the other side of the village, after nearly a quarter of a mile, the road takes a sudden left 'dog-leg'. After another 200 yards, you are on the attack line of the 17/King's on 1 July. To your left is the area where the 20/King's attacked and to your right, that of the French 153e R.I.. At this point, it is interesting to note the topography of the battlefield all around you, as it has changed very little since 1916. To the far left is Talus Boisé and to the near left is Machine Gun Wood. It was between these two woods that 21 Brigade made its attack.

Immediately ahead is Germans Wood, with the tip of Maricourt Wood on the right. Ahead of you, in the distance are Bernafay and

Original dug out iron opposite Maricourt Church.

The photograph below illustrates the strength of German dugouts which were made as safe and as permanent as possible.

Trônes Woods, but dominating, on the ridge to the left, is Montauban. It is not difficult to imagine how it must have looked to the Allied soldiers as they emerged, for the first time, from their trenches that morning. For even though a week's intensive shelling had reduced the enemy positions to pulp, the task of fighting uphill and capturing the heavily fortified village must have been a daunting one – especially to soldiers who up until then, had been conditioned to believe the golden rule of trench fighting – that you never put even your head above the parapet, let alone your whole body. If you continue up the road for about 100 yards, there is a turning to the left, which takes you down past Machine Gun Wood (La Garenne Simon on the modern maps). Just past the wood, the road turns through 90 degrees up to the right and peters out more or less in the attack line of the19/Manchesters. Before you turn the car around, you can check your position by looking up to the tip of Talus Boisé over to your left. No Man's Land was probably at its widest anywhere on XIII Corps' front, at this point.

Returning to your original position on the road from Maricourt to Montauban, if you drive for another quarter of a mile, you will notice that the ground has started to rise as you have driven across No Man's Land and have arrived in Favière Trench – the old German front line at this point. After nearly another quarter of a mile, you will draw level with Germans Wood (La Garenne Petit Charme), on your right and you are then roughly astride the German support line, known as Favière Alley. Germans Wood was captured, along with 30 prisoners, by A Company of the 17/King's, just before 8 am.

Half a mile later, as the road has reached its peak below Montauban itself, you are in the centre of the old fortified position known as Glatz Redoubt, captured by the 18/King's and 19/Manchesters, which allowed troops of the 16th and 17/Manchesters and the 2/Royal Scots Fusiliers of 90 Brigade, to move forward and take the village. Three hundred yards further on, if you look to your left you can clearly see

Montauban on the ridge with Germans Wood on the right.

The rear of the Glatz Redoubt from the old German lines. The hedge marks the entrances to original German dugouts. It was here, on 8 July, that Lt Colonel Trotter was mortally wounded.

Montauban from the Glatz Redoubt.

the hedgerow which was the old railway embankment which ran across the middle of the battlefield and gave Train Alley its name. Further over to the left, and slightly behind, the reverse slope of Glatz Redoubt can be seen, where the Germans had sited the entrances to their dug–outs, making them virtually impregnable to British fire.

In 1916, the area in front of Montauban was marked off by many hedges and it was behind these that German machine-gunners, snipers and bombers were able to shelter unseen. These hedges are remembered today on the modern French maps by the fact that the area just in front of the village is still called *Derrière les Haies* (behind the hedges). Immediately over to the right, at this point, the ruins of the sucrerie/briqueterie can be seen across the next field. The road into Montauban now becomes sunken and when it emerges into the village, you are at the Liverpool and Manchester Pals Memorial, with the cross-roads to the Bazentins and *Quarry Cemetery* opposite and over to the right.

Turn right at this point and at the next cross-roads, in about half a mile, turn right again onto the D 197 and drive toward Maricourt once more. After passing a trackway to Hardecourt-aux-Bois on the left, you reach a clump of trees on the right and a rough field with old stacks of hay in it. This is all that remains today of the sucrerie or sugar beet works, captured by the 20/King's. The briqueterie, or brick works was on the opposite side of the road, but none of this now survives.

Shattered German concrete emplacement in the remains of the Briqueterie at Montauban.

You are now making the circuit in the opposite direction from Tour One but it allows you to imagine the German perspective of the battlefield and see how well their engineers had chosen the high ground on the Montauban Ridge. Drive on to Maricourt and back out onto the D 938, to complete Tour Six.

The remains of the Sucrerie / Briqueterie

TOUR SEVEN

30th Division – Across Caterpillar Valley

Tour Seven is designed to take the traveller out of Montauban through Montauban Alley and across Caterpillar Valley to see not only what might have been possible had the 30th Division been allowed to exploit its advantage on the afternoon of 1 July 1916, but also to appreciate what the battle must have looked like from the German perspective. It is designed to be undertaken by car, bicycle, or on foot and is in two parts.

The first part of the tour begins alongside the Liverpool and Manchester Pals Memorial in Montauban, on the D 64, facing the direction of Mametz. Drive towards the church, L'Eglise Saint Giles, which is on the right and just before you get there, there is a turning to the right, opposite the building marked *'Salle Polyvolante de Montauban'*, which is the village function hall. The road is signposted *Rue de L'Eglise*. At the bottom of the road, after about 100 yards, take a left turn and as you pass between the two halves of a farm there, look to the left where there is a superb relic of the Great War – a compost enclosure made from German dug-out 'elephant iron'. On the right hand side of the road you can now clearly see Caterpillar Valley and the Bazentin Ridge. A couple of hundred yards later, as you reach the end of the metalled road surface, the road takes a severe right angled 'dog leg'. If you look to the left, at this point, there is a no entry sign *'A Tous Véhicules'* forbidding vehicles, which marks the entrance to a semi-sunken lane which goes back up into the village. This is the

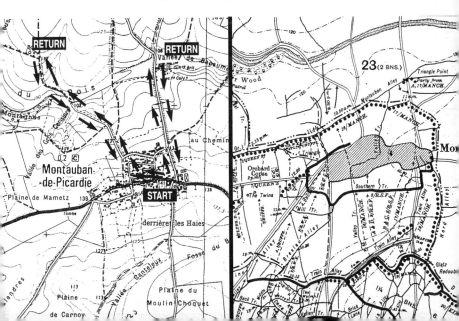

Original German dugout iron used to form a compost heap on a farm at Montauban.

remains of an original German communication trench which connected Montauban to Montauban Alley, (called Staubwasser Graben by the Germans) – the defensive/communications trench which ran from Pommiers Redoubt right around Montauban to the extreme eastern tip of the village.

If you drive down the 'dog leg', after about a hundred yards, you cross through the position where the road bisected Montauban Alley and roughly where men of the 16/Manchesters captured the German field guns of Feldartillerie-

British 'Plum Pudding' fuse plug found in Montauban Alley in February 1998. It must have belonged to a mortar fired at the Germans from that position after 1 July 1916.

Looking across Caterpillar Valley – the hedge marks the spot where Montauban Alley crossed the road.

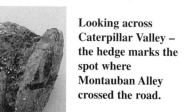

MONTAUBAN ALLEY

Regiment Nr. 21. Virtually nothing remains of the Alley today except for a small hedge on the right of the road at this point, which contains debris and remains from trench fortifications and leads off to the north east and eventually round the village. The road begins to drop to the floor of Caterpillar Valley just after this point, which also confirms the position of Montauban Alley as it is the last of the high ground north of Montauban and the last point where a defensive stand might have been made. Instead of defending it, however, it was abandoned as the Germans fled from Montauban across the valley and up to the safety of Bazentin le Grand.

When you finally reach the floor of the valley, after about half a mile, on your left is Caterpillar Wood, heavily fortified by the Germans before the 1 July assault and entered briefly by the patrol from the 8/Norfolks, who had come along Caterpillar Trench from Montauban Alley. If you continue to drive past the wood the road begins to rise until it peters out at the edge of a small wood. This wood is called Bois Leclerc but in 1916, the British called it Marlborough or Marlboro Wood. Then, it was heavily fortified by German infantry and artillery as it was the last defence against an attack up the valley to the Bazentin Ridge. If you turn round here, pause before making your way back down into the valley again, to see how Montauban dominates the ridge and how the battlefield would have looked to the Germans before 1 July. You can see quite clearly the hedge which marks Montauban Alley and get a good perspective of the furthest advance made by the 30th Division on that day. Return now, back along the road to the Liverpool and Manchester Pals Memorial.

Without stopping and driving at a steady 30 m.p.h., (45 k.p.h.) it should have taken you approximately eight minutes there and back covering about two miles. Walking, and bearing in mind the steepness of the valley sides, it should have taken approximately one hour.

For the second half of Tour Seven, begin, as before, at the Liverpool and Manchester Pals Memorial, but this time facing in the direction of Guillemont. Drive around the circular rose garden in the middle of the road and take the road almost opposite the memorial, marked by the Commonwealth War Graves Commission signpost *Quarry Cemetery*.

The road almost immediately begins to dip down into the valley and

Montauban on the ridge and Caterpillar Valley and part of the wood. This is how it would have looked to the Germans before the village was destroyed.

QUARRY CEMETERY

A view taken from former German positions showing Quarry Cemetery in the centre and the edge of Bernafay Wood on the left skyline and Montauban village on the right.

after a quarter of a mile, you have reached the final consolidated position for the gains made by midnight on the 1 July, by the 17/Manchesters. A further 200 yards down the road takes you to the position known as Triangle Point, at the spot where the road once more bisects Montauban Alley. This time, however, there is no sign of the old trenchworks, except that the road dips appreciably more steeply after this point. Triangle Point was reached by a party from A Company of the 17/Manchesters on the afternoon of 1 July, probably the most northern point reached by any troops in XIII Corps' area.

From there, there was a panoramic vista of the battlefield ahead and the view has changed little today. To the left are the Bazentins and their respective woods, immediately in front is the main road to the Bazentins and Quarry Cemetery. On the Bazentin Ridge, the D 20 road which connects Contalmaison with Longueval, can clearly be seen with Caterpillar Valley Cemetery over to the right. Beyond this is Longueval, with Delville Wood behind it. Drive a further quarter of a mile down into the valley floor again and stop and turn round at Quarry Cemetery. It was from the quarry on this site, (which gave the cemetery its name), that the Germans made the abortive counter-attack on Montauban at 9.30, on the evening of 1 July. Now drive back up the road towards the village and as you pass through Triangle Point once more, look to your left to see Bernafay Wood abandoned by the Germans after Montauban fell and then re-entered when they realised that the British had not taken it. Just beyond it is Trônes Wood. Once more enter Montauban and stop at the Liverpool and Manchester Pals Memorial.

Allowing for the unevenness of the road surface and the turn-round, the second part of Tour Seven is about one mile long and should take about three minutes by car, without stopping. On foot, however, and it is worth the effort for the view across the valley alone, it should take no more than half an hour.

Notes

1 See Chapter Four.
2 See Battleground Europe Series *Fricourt-Mametz, Somme,* by Michael Stedman.
3 See Chapter One.

Chapter Four

MEN, MEMORIALS AND MEMORIES

This chapter outlines the significant and interesting sites and memorials to be found today within and around the old XIII Corps boundaries. Each place is set out alphabetically for ease of finding and stories connected with the victorious soldiers of 1 July 1916 are told where appropriate. The numbers after each title refer to the map included in this chapter which makes it easier to find each location.

For cemetery visits, it is easiest to refer to The Commonwealth War Graves Commission/Michelin 1 : 200,000 map No. 52, with overprinted cemetery details. Where the dead of the successful attack on Montauban are concerned, it is odious to give prominence to any one man over another, for all played their own part in the ultimate victory. Where certain soldiers have been mentioned in the main texts, however, their details are shown where they are buried.

Bernafay Wood British Cemetery, Montauban (1)

Bernafay Wood British Cemetery is situated on the western side of the D. 197 Maricourt to Longueval road opposite the north west corner of the wood itself and is shown as Section 10, Cemetery No. 91, on CWGC/Michelin Map No. 52.

The wood fell to men of the 9th (Scottish) Division (which was in reserve on 1 July 1916) and the cemetery was begun next to a dressing station there, in August 1916 for casualties being brought back from the fighting of that month and afterwards, until April 1917. After the Armistice it was re-opened as a

KEY

Bernafay Wood British Cemetery, Montauban
The Boucher and Lepage Memorial
The Cochin Memorial
Carnoy Military Cemetery
Dantzig Alley British Cemetery, Mametz
The Liverpool and Manchester Pals Memorial
The Madonna of Montauban
The Maltz Horn Farm Memorial
The Monclin Memorial
). Péronne Road Cemetery, Maricourt
. Quarry Cemetery, Montauban
. The Trônes Wood Memorial to the 18th Division

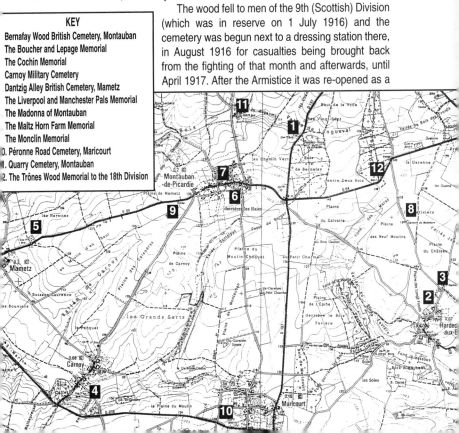

concentration burial site for the battlefields immediately east of Bernafay Wood and was also increased by 284 re-burials from Bernafay Wood North Cemetery, when the latter was closed down. Bernafay Wood North Cemetery was originally situated opposite the north end of the wood, on the eastern side of the road; the present cemetery contains 20 special memorials to soldiers know to have been buried in Bernafay Wood North, but whose graves were subsequently lost.

None of the dead buried in Bernafay Wood British Cemetery were actually killed in the assault on Montauban on 1 July 1916, but many of them were the liberators of the village, killed in later actions in the area, particularly during the fighting for nearby Trônes Wood.

Altogether, the remains of 922 soldiers are buried there, 793 from the United Kingdom, 122 from Australia, four from South Africa, two from New Zealand and one from India. In all 417 are unidentified.[1]

The Boucher and Lepage Memorial (2)

Although not strictly in the area captured by XIII Corps, but nevertheless part of the involvement of 1 July, is a memorial to two French soldiers of 153e R.I. It stands on the edge of a field up a track off the road which connects the outskirts of Hardecourt-aux-Bois with the south-eastern edge of Trônes Wood. Made from crumbling concrete, despite a fairly recent attempt at renovation, the memorial commemorates two soldiers of the 153e, Marcel Boucher and his friend Romeo Lepage who died together on that spot on 28 July 1916. The 153e, of course, were on the right of 89 Brigade of the 30th Division on 1 July and helped the Division in later battles of Maltz Horn Farm and Guillemont.

Soldat Marcel Boucher was born in Paris in the Seine Département on 13th May 1896 and his friend Caporal Roméo René Octave Jules Lepage was born one month later in Vert-Saint-Denis in the Département of Seine et Marne on 20 June 1896. After the war, Boucher's remains were exhumed and in November 1921 were returned to his family in Paris where they were re-buried in a private grave. Lepage's body was never recovered and identified, but it is presumed to be amongst the many unknown soldiers from his regiment whose bones lie in Ossuary No. 3, in the French National Cemetery at Albert.[2]

The Cochin Memorial (3)

Similarly not strictly in XIII Corps area, but likely to be encountered by a traveller to the area, is a memorial to Capitaine A. Cochin of 146e R.I., which is situated at the northern junction of the roads which connect the south-eastern edge of Trônes Wood and Guillemont with Hardecourt-aux-Bois, not far from the Boucher and Lepage Memorial.

It takes the form of a calvary made from wrought iron, dramatically set within four trees. The limbs of the cross are made to represent weapons of war and display shells and machine gun belts, the centrepiece being a soldier being taken aloft to heaven enfolded in the wings of an angel.

The inscription set on it, in two parts, translates as:

> The harder the ordeal, the more necessary it is to be there' 'Here Capitaine Augustin Cochin fell, killed in the attack of 8 July 1916. Wounded

three times, his arm broken, although disabled he returned to the battle for love of his country and his soldiers.

Capitaine Augustin Denis Marie Cochin was born in Paris in the Seine Département on 22 December 1876 and was thus nearly forty years old when he died so gloriously for his native land. No information is available concerning his final resting place.[2]

Carnoy Military Cemetery (4)

Carnoy Military Cemetery is situated on the western side of a slip road from the D. 938 Carnoy to Maricourt road just south of the village of Carnoy itself and is shown on Section 10, Cemetery No. 94, on CWGC/Michelin Map No. 52.

It was originally on the site of a small station on the Albert to Péronne light railway and was begun in August 1915 by the 2/King's Own Scottish Borderers and the 2/King's Own Yorkshire Light Infantry, of the 5th Division. After 1 July 1916, its numbers were swelled by dead brought there from various Field Ambulances and it was closed, as the fighting had moved on, in March 1917.

When the Germans took the area again in March 1918, they used it to bury some of their own dead (between the British graves and the entrance) and some British dead as well, before building their own cemetery alongside. The German dead in both the British and German cemeteries were removed in 1924, and re-buried at Fricourt and Carnoy German Cemetery was closed.

Today, Carnoy British Cemetery contains 837 graves. There are 828 United Kingdom dead buried there, five from New Zealand, two from Canada, one from Australia and one from South Africa. Twenty nine of the graves contain the bodies of unidentified soldiers. There are many burials of men from 53, 54 and 55 Brigades who were killed on 1 July 1916 or who died from wounds received in the attack on Montauban and later. [3]

Amongst the many dead heroes of 1 July buried in Carnoy Military Cemetery is Second Lieutenant Frank Gregson Rushton, of Darwen, Lancashire, commissioned into the 2/Wiltshire Regiment and attached to the 53rd Trench Mortar Battery. It was he who was killed by the sniper in Montauban Alley, who in turn was finally silenced by Company Sergeant Major Sayer of the 6/Royal Berkshires. Another soldier buried there, perhaps better known, is Captain W.P. Nevill of the 8/East Surreys and 'footballs' fame.

Wilfred Percy Nevill, always known as 'Bill' or 'Billie', was born on 14 July 1894 in London, one of the nine children of Thomas George and Elizabeth Ann Nevill, seven of whom survived to adulthood. He was educated at Dover College and then in 1913, went up to Jesus College, Cambridge to read Classics. He never completed his degree, however, because within a year, the war interceded and he was quick to enlist. Having already been an enthusiastic member of Dover College Officers' Training Corps, he took to soldiering quite naturally and in November 1914 was gazetted Second Lieutenant in The East Yorkshire Regiment. By this time, Nevill was already thinking of making the Army his career, forsaking his earlier choice of schoolmaster and following a period of instruction at the Staff College in Camberley, he was eventually posted

Captain W P Nevill in 1914 in the uniform of the E. Surreys.

to the 8/East Surreys.

After training with the Battalion throughout the winter and spring of 1914/1915, he eventually arrived in France with the rest of the battalions of the 18th Division. Within six weeks of his arrival, with obvious approval for his new life, he had applied to be transferred to the Regular Army. He was a tall man – over six feet in height and although not conventionally handsome, he had a boyish charm which infected all that he met. At school and university he had excelled at sport and displayed a high level of intelligence. He was also possessed of a huge 'public school' style sense of humour – sometimes inclined to border on the childish! One often reads of officers in the Great War being beloved by their men – particularly in obituaries of dead officers, – but in Nevill's case it seems to have been true – everyone really liked him. One who knew him well, Sergeant Cutting, wrote to Nevill's mother in this vein, after her son's death:

> *I do trust you will not think this a liberty, but – though I was only a Sergeant and your son a Captain – I can safely say he was my friend.*

> *Therefore I feel that, as one who knew him well ..... I must write just a few lines & tell you how we all loved him.*[4]

Long before the attack on 1 July, Nevill and his brother officers realised the strain a frontal assault on the enemy's trenches would present to men used to sheltering well below a trench parapet. Nevill himself was of the opinion that the usual tot of rum given at 'Stand To' and before an attack, endowed the wrong kind of false courage. Thus he conceived the plan to allow his men to dribble footballs across No Man's Land when the time came – simply to calm them and take their minds away from what could become, for them, the worst possible outcome. Having discussed this with the commanding officer of the 8/East Surreys, Major, (acting Lieutenant Colonel) A.P.B. Irwin,[5] on his next leave to England Nevill purchased some footballs. Accounts vary as to how many were actually taken back to France, but family sources stated that only three were purchased and only two of them were ever taken to the Somme.[4] Popular accounts written at the time, but not necessarily based on fact, assumed that there had been four in all, one for each platoon in B Company, which Nevill commanded. A prize was also offered for the platoon which first scored a 'goal' in the German trenches. Some accounts state that it was a £1 treasury note – paper promissory notes had recently been introduced as a war measure instead of gold sovereigns.

On the eve of the battle, two footballs were printed with the messages: '*The Great European Cup-Tie Final. East Surreys V Bavarians. Kick off at zero*' and '*No Referee*'. The latter was a reference to the fact that no rules of play were to be observed.

As we have already seen in Chapter Two, when 'zero' arrived, Nevill himself kicked one of the footballs into No Man's Land to begin the '*Great European Cup-Tie Final*'. He seems to have made it across No Man's Land and was shot through the head as he reached the German wire. Outlined so obviously as an officer by his uniform and his magnificent leading example, he would have been an obvious target for the German gunners Seven of the 8/East Surreys' officers were killed in the attack including Nevill's Company second in command, Lieutenant R.E. Soames, who had kicked-off the other football.

Their bodies were recovered from the battlefield and were buried together in Carnoy Military Cemetery, almost a mile and a half away, on the afternoon of 3 July. There they still all lie today, in Row E – six out of the seven in three graves, probably because of the shortage of burial places at the time – the burial parties not knowing exactly how many more casualties the battle would bring Only Captain Nevill has his own headstone – which bears the cap badge of his commissioned unit – The East Yorkshire Regiment and not his beloved 8/East Surreys, because he was still officially only *attached* to the Kingston-on-Thames battalion.

The two footballs were also recovered, on 2 July, in the German wire and immediately assumed the rôle of precious relics. By the middle of July the British press had featured the heroics of the footballs story and lauded it as an example of British sportsmanship under the most trying of conditions. With the casualty figures for the battle beginning to show the public that the 'Great Push' was in fact no such thing, any piece of news which showed steadfastness under fire and the British spirit of fair play in adversity was immediately seized upon.

The Germans too, seized upon it, however, but for exact opposite reasons! Re-publishing themselves the specially commissioned drawing of the incident, by *Illustrated London News* artist R. Caton Woodville, they used it to show how stupid the English were. Their view was that rather than taking the war seriously, the English preferred to see the whole thing as a childish game and as such, could never hope to win!

Overall, however, the British view of the incident is the one which has prevailed. It was best exemplified by the return of one of the recovered footballs, deflated and wrapped in sacking, probably from a sand bag, to the Regimental Depôt at Kingston-on-Thames, on the evening of 20 July. The following morning, a special parade was held by Lieutenant-Colonel H.P. Treeby, DSO, the Depôt commander, when all available troops were formed up in a hollow square, facing a table bearing the Union flag and the football, still wrapped in its sacking. By coincidence, one of the 'footballers', Private A.W. Draper of the machine-gun section, who was wounded in the action, was present – he had gone to the Depôt to replace his blood-stained tunic. Lieutenant-Colonel H.P. Treeby addressed the assembled troops thus:

> *Officers, N.C.O.s and Comrades - I have assembled you before me this morning that you may share with me the witnessing of the opening of this parcel, containing the historic football of the East Surrey Regiment which arrived at the Depôt last night. On that ever-to-be-memorable 1st July 1916 the day of the great French and British advance for which we have waited and worked for nearly two years, our gallant 8th Battalion, under the command that day of Major Irwin advanced to the attack on Montauban. It was the scene of the heaviest fighting and the Battalion was opposed by the Prussian Guard [sic] .*

> *As is now well known, the Battalion was led out of the British trenches by Captain Nevill and the signal for the advance was his kicking-off the football contained in this parcel. With splendid gallantry this and other footballs were dribbled up under the withering fire right into the German lines.*

147

One of only two remaining footballs kicked across No Man's Land on 1 July by the 8 East Surreys. This one is held in the Princess of Wales's Royal Regimental Museum at Dover Castle. Princess of Wales's Royal Regimental Museum

The other surviving football now held in The Queen's Royal Surrey Regimental Museum in Guildford.

In the early days of the war the nation could not be aroused to see the danger of an invasion. ..... Young men still played their football matches on our fields while large crowds looked on and cheered. ..... We called upon them to come forward and play the larger game ..... and they have played the nobler game in the defence of our country and our families. ..... The football fields have become the battlefields of France, of Flanders, of Egypt, Gallipoli and Mesopotamia and today we are reminded by this football of how splendidly that game has been played.

At no small cost has this football been dribbled up into the German trenches. It cost the 8th Battalion that day, in killed and wounded, 14 officers, 525 N.C.O.S and men, a total of all ranks of 539, and the gallant officer who kicked this football off, fell himself in front of the German trenches. The care of this sacred emblem of the 8th Battalion's devotion and heroism has been entrusted to me by its Commanding Officer. In affectionate memory we shall lay it up, and in years to come it will be a fitting memorial to the sacrifice of the gallant Battalion of this Regiment who played the game so well on that eventful day and who served so faithfully their God and King and Country.[6]

At the conclusion of the Colonel's speech, the ball was unwrapped and to the cheers of the assembled company, Private Draper was called forward to inflate it, after which it went on public display.

Incredibly, both the Montauban footballs still survive, one in the Regimental Museum of The Princess of Wales's Royal Regiment and Queen's Regiment at Dover Castle and the other in The Queen's Royal Surrey Regimental Museum at Guildford. Perhaps the words of Lieutenant-Colonel H.P. Treeby were prophetic, for they have indeed become, *'a fitting memorial to the sacrifice of the gallant Battalion of this Regiment who played the game so well on that eventful day and who served so faithfully their God and King and Country.'*

Perhaps, however, the final word on Captain Nevill and his famous action that day should be left to Sergeant Cutting:

Your son was a brave man he was a good man. He made us better men for having known him.[4]

Dantzig Alley British Cemetery, Mametz (5)

Dantzig Alley British Cemetery is situated on the northern side of the main D 64 road from Mametz to Montauban and is shown on Section 9, Cemetery No. 86, on CWGC/Michelin Map No. 52.

It is so called because it was on the site of the German Danzig Alley trench system, the remains of which still exist on the other side of the road opposite the main gate.[7] It was begun after the fighting of 1 July was over, by Field Ambulances front line units and graves registration units who utilised the trenches already dug by the Germans. After the Armistice it was greatly enlarged as a concentration cemetery from the nearby battlefields north and east of Mametz and, as a result, although not strictly within XIII Corps attack area for the first day of the Somme battle, many of its dead are buried there, from both the 18th and 30th Divisions.

Many of these dead had already been buried in small battlefield cemeteries in 1916 and their remains subsequently lost and they are commemorated on special memorials in the cemetery. Others, whose remains were re-buried, were taken from Aeroplane Cemetery, Fricourt, Bottom Wood Cemetery, Fricourt, Bulgar Alley Cemetery, Mametz, Hare Lane Cemetery, Fricourt, Mametz German Cemetery, Mametz, Mansel Copse Cemetery, Mametz, Mansel Copse West Cemetery, Mametz, Montauban Road Cemetery, Carnoy and Vernon Street Cemetery, Carnoy, when these small cemeteries were closed.

As well as the graves, there is also a memorial to the 14/Royal Welsh Fusiliers of the 38th (Welsh) Division, placed there in 1929 by former comrades in memory of those who fought and died in the area, especially in Mametz Wood.

Altogether, there are 2,035 graves in the cemetery; 1,922 from the United Kingdom, seventeen from New Zealand, thirteen from Australia, ten from Canada and three from South Africa. At the end of the war there were also five French graves and seven German, but they have since been moved to their own national cemeteries in the area.[8]

Amongst the graves of many heroes of 1 July 1916 is that of Lieutenant William Howard Savage of the 11/Royal Fusiliers, whose part in the attack on Pommiers Redoubt ensured the success of its capture. He was the son of William F. and Edith M. Savage of 70, Park Drive, Port Elizabeth, South Africa.

The Liverpool and Manchester Pals Memorial (6)
On the eastern edge of Montauban village on the D. 64, almost opposite the road to Bazentin le Grand and Longueval (signposted *Quarry Cemetery*), stands the Liverpool and Manchester Pals Memorial. It is in the form of a small obelisk bearing the cap badges and names of the Liverpool and Manchester Pals Battalions who captured the village on 1 July 1916 and the inscription in English and French:

The idea for a memorial there was conceived as far back as 1972, when the

TO THE GLORIOUS MEMORY OF THE LIVERPOOL AND MANCHESTER PALS WHO AS PART OF THE 30TH DIVISION LIBERATED THIS VILLAGE 1 JULY 1916	A LA MÉMOIRE DE NOS GLORIEUX CAMARADES DE LIVERPOOL ET DE MANCHESTER QUI ONT LIBÉRÉ CE VILLAGE AVEC LA 30 EME DIVISION LE 1 ER JUILLET 1916

author made his first pilgrimage to the Somme. Having nurtured a life-long interest in the Liverpool Pals, he was surprised to discover that there was no memorial anywhere in Britain or on the Continent to what he regarded as a very special breed of people.

Following the publication of his book Liverpool Pals [9] in 1991, he was given the impetus to do something to rectify this omission and, with the help of The Merseyside Branch of the Western Front Association, he set about commissioning memorials in Belgium, France and Great Britain. Following the unveiling of a brass plaque in St. George's Memorial Church in Ypres and the restoration of the four original Colours of the Liverpool Pals Battalions in Liverpool, which had been rotting in Liverpool Town Hall, he decided that the most important memorial should be in Montauban, to commemorate the Liverpool Pals Battalions of the 30th Division and their successes of 1 July 1916.

Having decided on a design roughly based on a memorial stone in Dantzig Alley Cemetery, he then suggested it to WFA branch members Peter Threlfall and Derek Sheard, who sketched and designed the plans for the memorial. Fund raising was then undertaken in a big way, the designing and selling of a set of commemorative postal covers by Derek Sheard, raising a significant proportion of the money. Having found that the Commonwealth War Graves Commission was too busy to help in the actual execution of the memorial, the services of a Péronne firm of stone masons – the Bobeuf Family – was then enlisted and given the design, to be executed in Portland stone.

Before all this was possible, however, the permission of the people of Montauban and the purchasing of a suitable piece of land in the village were both vital. With the help of Tom and Janet Fairgrieve of Delville Wood, at Longueval, on the Somme, contact was made with Monsieur Gilbert Froment, the mayor of Montauban and his deputy, Monsieur Gérard Driencourt-Brule. Not only did they seek and gain the permission of the people of the village, on behalf of the appeal fund, but Monsieur Driencourt generously gave some of his land to the project, right on the main D. 64 road.

At this stage, it was decided to include the Manchester Pals Battalions in the memorial, for several reasons. Firstly, as we have seen, it was mainly through the efforts of the men from both these great north-western cities that the village was captured – The Liverpool Pals with others, took and held the German front and reserve lines and the Manchester Pals, with others, took and held the village itself. Secondly, The Liverpools and the Manchesters had amalgamated in 1958 to form one regiment, The King's Regiment, so not to commemorate both would not only have been inappropriate, but plainly ludicrous! This proved to be a most sensible decision, not least because of the invaluable help the appeal fund received from The King's Regiment and its old comrades associations.

Having overcome many problems on the way – the fund-raising was probably the easiest – the culmination of everybody's efforts was the unveiling of the memorial on 1 July 1994 at approximately 12.30 p.m. – more or less the time that the Briqueterie fell to the 20/King's, which marked the fall of the whole of Montauban.

Having been promised the regimental band of The King's Regiment, 'Options for

Change' defence cuts disbanded this unit twenty four hours before the ceremony was due and similarly the French 153e R.I. (whom it was hoped would attend in force), was disbanded two months earlier. However, when the day arrived, the King's Regiment's contacts had worked miracles and not only was there an excellent British band – that of The Royal Air Force, Germany – but an equally excellent French Army band – quite unexpected by anyone on the day, – from the 43e R.I.. All the troops on the day were brilliantly marshalled by WFA branch member Les Bodicoat, who was equally at home with generals, airmen, mayors and clergymen!

Conjoined British and French national flags covered the memorial as the ceremony began and after speeches in English and French, it was unveiled by General Sir Peter Davies of the British Army, before the Last Post was played by a bugler from 5/8 King's Regiment.

The whole ceremony was witnessed by up to four hundred people including those already involved, villagers, holiday makers and the military of Great Britain and France. Although it took nearly eighty years before the feat of arms of the Lancashire men of the 30th Division on 1 July 1916 was recognised, perhaps this feat will now be remembered well into the 21st Century.

The Madonna of Montauban (7)

Inside the Church of St. Giles in the centre of Montauban is the only remaining official relic of the battle for the village. Unless the church is open, the visitor will have to seek the door key from the Mairie – the town hall – next to the church.

Inside, on a special stand at the front right of the church, is a stone head of the Virgin Mary. Originally, the whole statue – the figure of the Virgin with outstretched arms, stood outside the church and survived the British bombardment prior to the capture of the village. Some time after this, however, it must have been hit and broken apart by German shell fire, the head remaining more or less complete.

This head was then discovered by a British officer, taken from the village back to Britain as a souvenir, and later given by him to a friend. At some time in its post-Great War existence, it was mounted on a wooded plinth which was inscribed:

THE MONTAUBAN MADONNA
BATTLE OF THE SOMME
1916

The Mayor of Montauban Gilbert Froment (left) and the Deputy Mayor, Gérard Driencourt (right) with 'The Madonna of Montauban'.

The friend kept it in her library and upon her death it was inherited by a Miss Valerie Ives of Netherby in Cumbria. In April 1986, she decided that its rightful place was back in Montauaban and she contacted Monsieur Gilbert Froment, the Mayor of Montauban, who was naturally delighted to hear from her. Eventually, in November 1986 she brought the Madonna's head back to Montauban where it was restored to its rightful place in the re-built church.

Just inside the main door of the church, on the right, there is also a plaque which commemorates fifteen soldiers and eight civilians from the village, who lost their lives in the Great War.

The Maltz Horn Farm Memorial (8)

On the roads which connect the south-eastern edge of Trônes Wood with Hardecourt-aux-Bois, is another outstanding memorial which although having no direct connection with the events of 1 July and XIII Corps is nevertheless worthy of inspection. It is the site of the former Ferme Malzkorn Duclercq, known to the British as Maltz Horn or Maltzhorn Farm.

The monument takes the form of an impressive calvary which dominates the ridge upon which it stands. On its base is the inscription:

ICI S'ELEVAIT LA FERME
MALTZKORN DUCLERCQ
DÉTRUITE PAR LES COMBATS
ACHARNES QUI FURENT
LIVRÉ A CET ENDROIT DU
1ER JUILLET AU 9 AOUT 1916

This translates as:

Here stood Maltzkorn Duclerq Farm, destroyed in the desperate battles which took place on this spot from 1 July to 9 August 1916.

Maltz Horn Farm, because of the height of the land on which it stood was an important feature of the landscape in July 1916 and Maltz Horn Trench jutted out like a small salient from the German defences at the farm. It was vital to the success of the Battle of Guillemont which began on 30 July 1916 that the farm fell and it was taken in the early morning of the attack, in a joint move by 1 July veterans the 2/Bedfords of 89 Brigade and the French 153e R.I..

Then only ruined and devastated buildings remained of the farm and it was never re-built after the Great War, the calvary being the only clue that it ever existed.

The Monclin Memorial (9)

On the D. 64 road from Mametz to Montauban on the left hand side of the road, just before Montauban is reached, there is a memorial in the form of a grey granite cross with the following inscription:

A LA MEMOIRE DE
HENRI THIERION DE MONCLIN
CAPITAINE DU 69e R. D'INFANTERIE

ET DES SOLDATS
DE LA 3e COMPAGNIE
MORTS POUR LA FRANCE
LE 28 SEPTEMBRE 1914

The site of the cross is where Montauban's former windmill used to stand and was the highest point of the village. As such, it would have been a vital point to hold and explains why Monclin and his men deemed it vital to fight and die there. Four years of shelling during the Great War reduced the spot to virtually nothing, however and when the fields were re-ploughed after the war most of the height was lost.

As we have already seen in Chapter One, Henri Thierion de **The Monclin Memorial.**
Monclin and his men were killed there, trying to hold back the Germans on the morning of 28 September 1914. His death was described later, somewhat poetically, by one of his comrades in the History of the Regiment.[10]

He was a fine chap, that Monclin, one of the purest souls of our regiment. Having already been wounded once with a bullet in the arm, in the fighting of August 1914 and evacuated to Bordeaux, he hurried his return to combat. The town where he was being tended presented too cruel a contrast for him – having seen suffering, pleasure seemed odious. Hastening from the rear without being fully recovered, he wanted to take up his place again in the fray. Everyday he would go down the lines as far as the first aid post to have his wound dressed - the trench and the battlefield – they were his hospital!

In Montauban, the company he commanded was up in the front line. The enemy attacked with fury. On the left and the right, (the French) were withdrawing, but he had not received any orders. He would die at his post!

In a familiar fashion, he shared some bars of chocolate, with his men. 'It's over – we won't need any provisions', he said. Then he made a large sign of the cross and invited the company to do the same. 'My children', he cried, 'Our mission is to hold on here. We will stay until we die. Let those who believe in God, pray.'.

He took up the gun of a dead man and fired it like a soldier. A bullet hit him in the shoulder and as he went away to be bandaged, he still tried to take aim – he did not even think!'

The enemy was gaining ground. A subaltern talked of retreat. The irrepressible captain threatened to beat his brains in, but he was so gentle he would never have hurt anyone.

He still had enough strength to seize his binoculars to observe. A second bullet laid him dead!

It is just possible that the remains of Henri Thierion de Monclin are buried under the granite cross, as the Ministère des Anciens Combattants et Victimes de Guerre, in Paris, the French equivalent of the Commonwealth War Graves Commission, does not have any burial details at all for this officer. Furthermore, on the IGN map of the area, the position is marked with the word *'Tombe'*, not the more usual *'Monument'* or *'Mémorial'* where only a commemoration is involved.

Péronne Road Cemetery, Maricourt (10)

Péronne Road Cemetery is situated on the north side of the D. 938 Carnoy to Maricourt road, just inside the village of Maricourt itself and is shown on Section 10, Cemetery No. 96, on CWGC/Michelin Map No. 52.

It was first created before 1 July 1916 by engineers of the 30th Division to bury the expected dead from the forthcoming attack. Private Steele of the 18/King's had first spotted it before the battle:

> Before the 1st of July, our fellows dug two big trenches, and they said they were for water, but I believe, – I was told afterwards, – that that was where they piled the dead, for the time being, like sardines. ..... It was on the left hand side of the road to Carnoy – they told us they were reserve water tanks.! [9]

Many front line units and Field Ambulances operating in the area after 1 July used the cemetery until its first closure in August 1917, when the war had moved on and there are also a few graves in the cemetery from 1918, when the war moved back. Originally it was named Maricourt Military Cemetery No. 3, and after the Armistice it was greatly enlarged by battlefield recoveries and reburials from smaller cemeteries in the immediate area. These were: Authuile Communal Cemetery Extension; Briqueterie East Cemetery, Montauban; Carnoy Communal Cemetery Extension; Casement Trench Cemetery, Maricourt; Fargny Mill French Military Cemetery, Curlu; La Cote Military Cemetery, Maricourt; Maricourt French Military Cemetery; Montauban Road French Military Cemetery, Maricourt and Talus Boisé British Cemetery, Carnoy.

Today, the cemetery contains 1,321 graves, 1,272 from the United Kingdom; thirty-four from South Africa, fourteen from Australia and one from Canada. Amongst this number are 366 unidentified graves and there are also twenty-six special memorials to soldiers who are known or believed to be buried in the cemetery.[11]

Many of the 30th Division who died in the struggle for Montauban are buried in the cemetery as well as many more who were killed in subsequent battles in the immediate area. One of these, who played a prominent rôle in the capture of Montauban, is Lieutenant-Colonel Edward Henry Trotter, DSO, commanding officer of the 18/King's. He was killed on the afternoon of 8 July, when a German shell landed right in the entrance of a former German dug-out in Glatz Redoubt which was being used as 21 Brigade Headquarters.

Lt. Col. E H Trotter

Lieutenant-Colonel Trotter's servant, Private Charles Arthur 'Charlie' Boosey, is buried not far away from him in the same plot. Aged twenty at his time of death, Charles Boosey came from Kirkdale, a suburb of Liverpool, where he lived with his parents. The same German shell which killed his Colonel also killed Second Lieutenant N.A.S. Barnard, Private Boosey and one other private and mortally wounded the commanding officer of the 18/Manchesters, Lieutenant-Colonel W.A. Smith.[12] The records of the Commonwealth War Graves Commission erroneously state that Boosey was killed the following day, however.

It was only some time after Boosey's death that a remarkable story emerged involving Captain J.H. Worthington, who had commanded A Company of the 16/Manchesters in the attack on Montauban. Worthington had been badly wounded in the assault, in the right lung, left hand and thigh. Whilst lying on the battlefield, he had been discovered by Boosey who was almost certainly reconnoitring the situation for his Colonel. The story is best told by Boosey's father Mr. Z. Boosey over the course of the next two years. It began with a letter to Captain Worthington written on 18 January 1917:

Dear Sir,

Would you please inform me if you are the Captn. Worthington wounded in Somme Battle July 1st who gave his glasses and an ox tongue to a Private of the King's L'pool Regt, if so I would like to write further to you,

Yours most faithfully

Z Boosey.

Hubert Worthington replied in the affirmative and ten days later received a more informative letter from the grieving father.

Dear Sir,

to make you understand everything, I think it best to make a general statement. My son was killed on the Somme July 8th last. In due course we received from the War Office, a wallet containing photos and a small diary. An entry in the diary reads thus, 'Captn Worthington of the Manchesters gave me an ox tongue and his glasses' . The item aroused my curiosity and I wrote to his pal to see if he could enlighten me on it.

He wrote me to this effect. Charlie came across Captn Worthington badly wounded and in a very exhausted condition. He dressed his wounds and made him as comfortable as circumstances would allow, this was under very heavy shell fire and as a mark of esteem he gave him his glasses.'

Now, Sir, as a parent, the statement greatly impressed me, as it was a tribute to his young manhood and the last action I heard of him doing in this world. I have endeavoured to get those glasses without success, not for the value of them, as an article they are useless to me. I was still making enquiries for them, since my object in writing to you was to find out if they had any distinguishing marks on them. I wasn't aware at the time you prized the glasses and nothing would give me greater happiness now, than to be able to forward them to you, which I most assuredly will do, if I am fortunate enough to trace them.

I hope I have made everything quite plain to you, Sir, also would you like me to continue my enquiries for them.

Yours Most Faithfully,

Z. Boosey.

Captain Worthington applied in the affirmative and then heard nothing more until a letter finally arrived for him written on 26th July 1918, over two years after the incident had occured:

Dear Sir,

The field glasses you gave to my son on the battle field in July 1916 came into my possession yesterday, having been forwarded by the Adjt of 18th Kings L'pool Regt.

'It would give me great pleasure to forward them, on hearing from you. I had despaired of ever getting them, but am more than satisfied, now that the enquiries made have produced such a good result.

Yours Faithfully

Z. Boosey'

Eventually, Hubert Worthington received his field glasses, which naturally became a treasured family possession thereafter.[13]

Another grave worthy of note in the cemetery, from 1918, is that of Lieutenant Colonel William Herbert Anderson VC, of the 12/Highland Light Infantry, who won his coveted decoration posthumously at nearby Faviere Wood, on 25 March 1918.

Further along the D. 938 on the north-east side of the crossroads at the junction of the Carnoy to Maricourt and the Suzanne to Montauban roads there stood a brewery before the Great War. Once this had been destroyed by the shelling a French cemetery named Ferme Caudron replaced it which was taken over by the British in August 1915 and renamed Maricourt Military Cemetery. It was used until Maricourt Military Cemetery No. 3 was opened for the casualties of the Somme battle. Then, after the Armistice, the bodies from this cemetery were moved to Cerisy-Gailly Military Cemetery, on the south bank of the Somme river.[14]

Other cemeteries in the Somme area which contain dead of the 18th and 30th Divisions from the 1 July fighting are Combles Communal Cemetery Extension and Heilly Station Cemetery, at Méricourt-l'Abbé. Of course those killed in the assault on Montauban whose bodies were never found and identified or whose graves were subsequently lost are commemorated on the Memorial to the Missing at Thiepval.

Quarry Cemetery, Montauban (11)

Quarry Cemetery is situated on the eastern side of the road which connects Montauban with Bazentin le Grand, on the floor of Caterpillar Valley and is shown on Section 10, Cemetery No. 90, on CWGC/Michelin Map No. 52.

As its name implies it is on the site of a former quarry and it was from this spot that the Germans of 6. Bayerisches Reserve Infanterie-Regiment and others, formed up for the abortive counter-attack on the 16th and 17/Manchesters in Montauban, at 9.30 pm, on the evening of 1 July. After Montauban had fallen, an advanced dressing station was set up in the quarry and those who died there formed the basis of the cemetery.

When the area fell once more to the Germans in March 1918, they used it for the burial of some of their own dead. The area was re-captured by the 18th Division, on 25 August 1918 and after the Armistice it was increased in size by the addition of burials of battlefield retrievals (almost all from July to December 1916) and the re-burials of bodies from Caterpillar Wood Cemetery No. 2, Green Dump Cemetery and Quarry Scottish Cemetery, all of which were closed down at the time.

It now contains the bodies of 731 soldiers 648 from the United Kingdom, thirty-six from New Zealand, twenty-five from Australia; six from South Africa; one Frenchman and fifteen Germans. None of these were killed during the assault on Montauban, but some of the liberators of the village are buried there, having been killed in subsequent battles. Some 158 bodies in the cemetery remain unidentified.[15]

The Trônes Wood Memorial to the 18th Division (12)

In a clearing just in front of Trônes Wood on the D. 64 from Montauban to Guillemont, is a large obelisk mounted on five stone steps, dedicated to the 18th Division. It has four sides and bears a bronze panel on the front, which has the embossed inscription:

TO THE GLORY OF GOD
AND
IN IMPERISHABLE MEMORY
OF THE
OFFICERS, N.C.Os. & MEN
OF THE
18TH DIVISION
WHO FELL FIGHTING FOR THE SACRED CAUSE
OF LIBERTY, IN THE
SOMME BATTLES OF 1916 AND 1918

Underneath this is then embossed:

THE GREATEST THING IN THE WORLD

followed by a verse from the scriptures.

Trônes Wood, known as Bois des Troncs or (Tree) Trunks Wood, to the French, was captured by the 18th Division on 14 July 1916 after fierce fighting. As we have already seen in Chapter Two, the 18th Division also helped liberate the same area on 25 August 1918. Other obelisks to the memory of the 18th Division are at Thiepval, on the Somme and on The Menin Road, in The Ypres Salient of Belgium.

Notes

1 *1914 – 1918 The War Dead of the Commonwealth, Bernafay Wood Cemetery,* Commonwealth War Graves Commission Register, France, No 400.

2 Ministère des Anciens Combattants, et Victimes de Guerre.

3 *1914 – 1918 The War Dead of the Commonwealth, Carnoy Military Cemetery,* Commonwealth War Graves Commission Register, France, No 513.

4 *Billie – The Nevill Letters,* by R.E. Harris – see the bibliography for full details.

5 See Chapter Two.

6 *The Surrey Comet,* 22 July 1916.

7 See Chapter Three.

8 *1914 – 1918 The War Dead of the Commonwealth, Dantzig Alley British Cemetery, Mametz,* Commonwealth War Graves Commission Register, France, No 397.

9 *Liverpool Pals* by G. Maddocks – see the bibliography for full details.

10 *Historique du 69e Régiment d'Infanterie,* published in 1928.

11 *1914 – 1918 The War Dead of the Commonwealth, Péronne Road Cemetery, Maricourt,* Commonwealth War Graves Commission Register, France, No 630.

12 Second Lieutenant Norman Arthur Southard Barnard is also buried in Péronne Road Cemetery; Lieutenant–Colonel William Alfred Smith, formerly second in command of the 20/King's died of his wounds on 9 July 1916. He is buried in Corbie Communal Cemetery Extension. Another casualty of the shell was the author's great-uncle, 16414 Sergeant Albert Edward Harry Gray of the 18/King's, who died of his wounds on 31st August 1916 at Le Havre. He is buried in Ste. Marie Cemetery, Le Havre.

13 The author is indebted to Crispin Worthington, Hubert Worthington's son, for the information contained in this section.

14 *1914 – 1918 The War Dead of the Commonwealth, Cerisy-Gailly Military Cemetery,* Commonwealth War Graves Commission Register, France, No 699.

15 *1914 – 1918 The War Dead of the Commonwealth, Quarry Cemetery, Montauban,* Commonwealth War Graves Commission Register, France, No 399.

BIBLIOGRAPHY

Books and Published Works

Atkinson C.T. - *The Queen's Own Royal West Kent Regiment, 1914 - 1919* (Simpkin, London 1924)

Banks T.M. Lieut-Col. and Chell R.A. Capt. - *With the 10th Essex in France* (Gay & Hancock, London, 1924)

Buchan J. - *The History of The Royal Scots Fusiliers (1678-1918)* (Nelson, London)

Chapman C., Cull I, Fox C., McIntyre M. and Webb L., - *On the Somme* (University of Reading, 1996)

Conan Doyle A. - *The British Campaigns in Europe (Bles,* London, 1928)

Davies F. and Maddocks G. - *Bloody Red Tabs* (Leo Cooper, London, 1995)

Edmonds J.E. Brig-Gen. Sir - *Military Operations France and Belgium 1916* (H.M.S.O. 1932)

Enser A.G.S. - *A Subject Bibliography of the First World War* (Deutsch, London, 1979)

Fraser-Tytler N. Lieut-Col. - *Field Guns in France,* (Hutchinson, London 1922)

Gliddon G. - *The Battle of the Somme - A Topographical History* (Sutton Publishing, Stroud 1997)

Harris R.E. - *Billie - The Nevill Letters* (Macrae 1991)

H.M.S.O. - *Officers Died in the Great War* (1919)

H.M.S.O. - *Soldiers Died in the Great War* (1922)

Hogg I.V. and Thurston L.F. - *British Artillery Weapons and Ammunition 1914-1918* (Ian Allan, London, 1972)

Holloway R. - *The Queen's Own Royal West Regiment* (Leo Cooper, London, 1973)

James Brig. E.A. - *British Regiments 1914-18* (Samson Books, London 1978)

Jarvis J.B and S.D. - *Officers Who Died in the Service of British, Indian and East African Regiments and Corps 1914-1919* (Roberts Medals, Reading, 1993)

Kempster F. Brig-Gen., and Westropp H.C.E. Brig-Gen., (Editors) - *Manchester City Battalions* (Sherratt and Hughes, Manchester, 1917)

Maddocks G.J. - *Liverpool Pals* (Pen and Sword, Barnsley, 1991)

Middlebrook M. - *The First Day on the Somme* (Lane, London, 1972)

Middlebrook M. and M. - *Somme* (Lane, London, 1995)

Mitchinson K.W. - *Pioneer Battalions in the Great War,* Leo Cooper, London,1997)

Moody R.S.H. Col. - *Historical Records of The Buffs East Kent Regiment* (Medici Society, London 1922)

Murphy C.C.R. Lieut-Col. - *The History of the Suffolk Regiment 1914-1927* (Hutchinson, London, 1928)

Nash D. - *German Infantry* 1914-1918 (Almark, London, 1971)

Nash T.A.M. (Editor) - *The Diary of an Unprofessional Soldier* (Picton Publishing, Chippenham, Wiltshire, 1991)

Nichols G.H.F. Capt. - *The 18th Division In the Great War* (Blackwood, Edinburgh and London, 1922)

Petre F.L. - *The History of the Norfolk Regiment 1685 - 1918* (Jarrold & Sons, Norwich)

Shepherd W.S. Maj. *The 2nd Battalion Wiltshire Regiment A Record of their Fighting in the Great War 1914-18* (Gale & Polden, Aldershot, 1927)

Stedman M. - *Manchester Pals* (Pen & Sword, Barnsley 1994)

Stephens F.J. and Maddocks G.J. - *Uniforms and Organisation of the Imperial German Army 1900-1918* (Almark, London, 1975)

Stanley F.C. Brig.-Gen. - *The History of the 89th Brigade 1914 - 1918* (Liverpool Daily Post, 1919)

Talbot-Booth Lieut-Cdr. E.C. - *The British Army Its History, Customs, Traditions and Uniforms* (Sampson Low, London, 1939)

The Times - *Diary & Index of the War* (Hayward & Son, Colchester, 1985)

Unknown - *Historique du 69e Régiment d'Infanterie,* (Paris, 1928)

Unknown - *Sixteenth : Seventeenth : Eighteenth : Nineteenth Battalions : The Manchester Regiment - A Record 1914-1918* (Sherratt & Hughes, Manchester, 1923)

Whalley-Kelly H. Capt. *'Ich Dien' The Prince of Wales's Volunteers (South Lancashire) 1914-1934* (Gale & Polden, Aldershot 1935)

Wise T. *A Guide to Military Museums and Other Places of Military Interest* (Imperial Press, Kighton, Powys, 1992)

Wylly H.C. Col. - *The Green Howards in The Great War* (Richmond, Yorkshire, 1926)

Wylly H.C. Col. - *History of The Queen's Royal Regiment, Volume VII.* (Gale & Polden, Aldershot)

Wyrall E. - *The Die-Hards In The Great War* (Harrison & Sons, London, 1926)

Newspapers and Journals

The Bedford Record, The Bedfordshire Times, The Bury Free Press, The Birkenhead News and Advertiser, The Bury and Norwich Post, The Eastern Daily Press, The Essex Chronicle, The Essex Weekly News, The Kent Messenger, The Kentish Gazette, The Liverpool Daily Post, The Liverpool Echo, The Norfolk Chronicle and Post, The Northampton Independent, The Norwich Mercury, The Surrey Advertiser and County Times, The Surrey Comet, The Wasp - Regimental Magazine of The Bedfordshire Regiment.

Non-Published Works

Herdman W.A. - *George Andrew Herdman : The Record of a Short But Strenuous Life* (Private Circulation, Liverpool, 1917)

War Diary *The 2nd Battalion The Bedfordshire Regiment*

War Diary *The 7th (Service) Battalion The Bedfordshire Regiment*

War Diary *The 8th (Service) Battalion The East Surrey Regiment*

War Diary *The 17th (Service) Battalion The King's (Liverpool Regiment)*

War Diary *The 18th (Service) Battalion The King's (Liverpool Regiment)*

War Diary *The 19th (Service) Battalion The King's (Liverpool Regiment)*

War Diary *The 20th (Service) Battalion The King's (Liverpool Regiment)*

War Diary *The 7th (Service) Battalion The Queens Regiment*

War Diary *The11th (Service) Battalion The Royal Fusiliers*

War Diary *The 2nd Battalion The Royal Scots Fusiliers*

War Diary *The 8th (Service) Battalion The Royal Sussex Regiment (Pioneers)*

War Diary *The 2nd Battalion The Wiltshire Regiment*